Dale
YO
GUIDE

Edited by
TERRY FLETCHER

Publishing Company Ltd

Dalesman Publishing Company Ltd
Stable Courtyard, Broughton Hall,
Skipton, North Yorkshire BD23 3AE

Text © 1994 Dalesman Publishing

Cover: York by Deryck Hallam

Printed by Hubbards

A British Cataloguing in Publication record is
available for this book

ISBN 1 85568 084 X

*While every effort has been made to ensure the
information given in this guide is accurate, we
recommend that you check before embarking on any
journey. Telephone numbers are given where known.*

CONTENTS

Malham Cove   *Derek Widdicombe*

Area covered by this guide

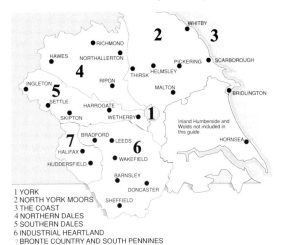

WHITBY

2

3

RICHMOND

HAWES

NORTHALLERTON

PICKERING SCARBOROUGH

4

THIRSK HELMSLEY

RIPON

INGLETON

5

MALTON

BRIDLINGTON

SETTLE

HARROGATE

Inland Humberside and
Wolds not included in
this guide

SKIPTON WETHERBY

1

HORNSEA

BRADFORD

7

LEEDS

6

HALIFAX

WAKEFIELD

HUDDERSFIELD

BARNSLEY

DONCASTER

SHEFFIELD

1 YORK
2 NORTH YORK MOORS
3 THE COAST
4 NORTHERN DALES
5 SOUTHERN DALES
6 INDUSTRIAL HEARTLAND
7 BRONTE COUNTRY AND SOUTH PENNINES

INTRODUCTION

by Terry Fletcher

Yorkshire could — and occasionally does — claim to be not so much a mere county as a complete country. If it were, then it would be the proverbial land of contrasts with the clichéd "something for everyone."

After all, the Broad Acres encompass two national parks, wild mountain country, sophisticated cultural centres, premier seaside resorts, peaceful villages and a capital that is arguably England's most historic city.

It has a classical literary heritage to rival any in Britain as well as being the setting for three of the country's favourite television series. It is the birthplace of eminent modern artists such as Henry Moore and David Hockney as well as being the home of that most populist icon, the saucy seaside postcard.

The Pennine valleys and northern cities were the crucible of the Industrial Revolution but now the towns which once reverberated to the clatter of clogs on setts bustle to the tread of tourists' feet.

The ancient attractions of York draw visitors from all over the world to marvel at the Minster and the wealth of medieval churches which still survive in the centre of the city. Historic buildings cluster in the narrow lanes and twisting alleys (or snickleways as they are known to the locals) that weave through its heart.

To the west are the former spa town of Harrogate, the historic miniature city of Ripon and the wide sweeps of the Yorkshire Dales. Long treasured by Yorkshiremen, this area — a national park for more than 40 years — has received a fresh influx of visitors from all over the world with the international success of the TV series All Creatures Great and Small. A sure way to irritate long-established Dales lovers is to refer to it as Herriot Country.

Nevertheless these are the valleys (especially in the north) of the James Herriot Books and though time

may have changed the vil-
lages, the landscape and its
spirit is little altered. The villages usually huddle protec-
tively in the valley bottoms
beside fast-flowing becks and
rivers. But the fells are often

**Yorkshire Dales
National Park**

empty except around honeypots like Malham and
Grassington or on the most popular walks such as the
demanding 26-mile Three Peaks circuit of
Ingleborough, Whernside and Penyghent.

The country's two most popular long distance
footpaths, the Pennine Way and the Coast to Coast
cross at Keld in Swaledale but all the Dales park is
walking country par excellence whether for gentle
riverside rambles or demanding rough country
yomps.

The smaller of the county's national parks, the
North York Moors, is dominated by vast open hori-
zons which in late summer become endless carpets of
purple heather. The view from their western escarpment across the Vale of York is spectacular while on
the ridges at the centre of the moors you can feel like
the last person left on earth.

The valleys here are gentler than their counterparts
in the Dales and the villages more blatantly picturesque with mellow stone or brick walls and red
pantiled roofs. The park is usually quieter than the
Dales though in spring the pilgrimage to see the
Farndale Daffodils — which locals will tell you were
the inspiration for Wordsworth's most famous poem
— can jam local roads. Even so the blooms are worth
the rise in blood pressure.

The area is also making its own belated bid for the

tele-tourists and parts of it are
now marketed as "Heartbeat
Country" after the police series
which is filmed at Goathland.
The park extends to the coast
where fishing villages like
Staithes and Robin Hood's Bay

Scarborough

snuggle into chinks in the cliffs which include some of the highest in England and provide spectacular high rise homes for millions of sea birds .

Running south is a string of towns and resorts, each with its own character. Whitby with its connections with Captain Cook and Dracula can be majestic, enchanting or spooky according to weather while just down the coast Scarborough bows to no one as Queen of the Coast. This is a resort with two huge beaches and the full panoply of tourist delights.

For decades it was the traditional holiday destination for thousands of Northern families, though the more adventurous alternated with Blackpool on the west coast. Further south Filey with its magnificent Brigg and Bridlington keep themselves more tightly laced and cast a slightly snooty eye at their northern neighbour. But these traditional holiday spots no longer have it all their own way and ironically are facing a challenge from the very towns which once provided their most staunch supporters.

The woollen towns of the Pennine Valleys —

"Summer Wine Country" for the square-eyed — are making their own pitch for the holidaymaker and Hebden Bridge and Holmfirth, as well as the established Bronte shrine at Haworth, now cater for visitors. Industrial heritage is the name of the game here with the mills reopened, many selling locally-produced craftware or relics of the region's industrial past. Canals which once brought industrial wealth now bring fresh supplies of visitors.

For the literary-minded, intent on pursuing Emily, Charlotte and Anne rather than Foggy, Compo and Clegg, no visit is complete without a trip round the Parsonage and a traipse across the moor to Top Withens, the prototype Wuthering Heights. The direction posts in Japanese bear silent testament to the international pulling power of Heathcliff and Cathy. Haworth Main Street bears anything but a silent witness to the selling power of the literary sisters.

Even the major cities, once content to be hives of industry and commerce are now setting out to attract visitors with major concert venues and arts festivals to back up museums and art galleries and revamped pedestrianised centres to lure the shopper.

Leeds boasts grand opera and a recently-built Henry Moore Gallery while just a dozen or so miles down the M1 the Yorkshire Sculpture Park at Bretton offers a chance to appreciate huge works in an outdoor "gallery" of a former stately home.

Unkind souls smirked at the likes of Bradford and Halifax as holiday destinations but the woollen capitals had the last laugh as the tourists flocked in. Bradford's jewel is the National Museum of Film and Photography where hands-on exhibits and film special effects enthral children of all ages. Halifax's Eureka Museum is another "hands-on" Mecca of discovery for children of all ages.

One secret still waiting to be discovered by mass tourism is the Yorkshire Wolds in what the planners like to call Humberside but which locals still call the East Riding. That is the part of the county we have left for the adventurous to explore for themselves.

▌ YORK

by John Scott

Y ork was a fascinating place to visit long before tourism arrived to gild the lily. There was always the Minster and the city's medieval walls wrapped around a cluster of narrow streets in which time had left intriguing traces of past inhabitants right back to Roman days.

There were old churches each a gem in its own right and reached by dozens of alleys or snickleways as they are known. And in keeping with the sleepy nature of the place its antiquities had that dry dusty look. It is so very different now. . .

Open top coaches ply the city with guides pointing out every nook and cranny, there are ghost walks down the snickleways, buskers in the squares and mushrooming museums hand out glossy literature that offers the visitor the latest historical 'experience' — be it Roman, Viking, Medieval, Georgian or

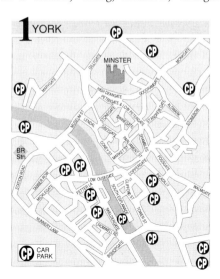

Victorian. Tourism now attracts 3m visitors a year to the city who pour £20m into the local economy.

But the essence of the city and its charm have survived all the slick publicity and marketing. The Minster still casts a benign spell and the medieval walls still provide the best free 'experience' of York with its semi-aerial views of pantiled roofs and church spires. The old buildings are no longer dusty and the narrow streets house bright new boutiques and tea shops.

York has become a bustling, cosmopolitan place — a living, working city which despite all the temptations has refused to turn itself into a museum. And yet every period of the city's long history has somehow managed to leave behind a solid memento of itself.

An antler worker in the recreated Viking street in the Jorvic Viking Centre, Coppergate.

Historical background

The Romans

Quintus Petillius Cerialis, the Roman Governor and at one time commander of the ill-fated 9th Legion, first put York on the map as Eboracum. He and his legions built a fortress with earth ramparts and wooden palisades at the joining of the rivers Ouse and Foss. Stone walls, streets and imposing public buildings soon followed. Constantine the Great was proclaimed Emperor here in the huge basilica parts of which can still be seen under York Minster. And it was from York that for a time the whole Roman world was governed.

The line of the old fortifications can be seen marked in pavements throughout the city and part of the fortress wall and a great defence tower surfaces in the Museum Gardens. For those determined to indulge in the ultimate Roman 'experience' there is a certain manhole cover in a certain street which when lifted enables you to crawl down a real Roman sewer (now provided with electric lights).

Anglo Saxon Times

The Anglo Saxons took over from the Romans in the fifth century and Eboracum became Eoferwic. The first cathedral of St. Peter was founded in 627 when Edwin, king of Northumbria became a Christian. Alcuin the scholar became Master of the School of St. Peter at York, later becoming master of Charlemagne's school at Aachen.

An Anglican tower — part of the Anglo Saxon restoration of the city defences — was found in modern times hidden in the medieval ramparts behind the York City Library.

Viking Times

The smelly, rubbish-laden streets of Viking York — or Jorvik as the battle axe wielding warriors called the city — were found in Coppergate during excavations between 1976 and 1981. Wooden house walls standing nearly six feet high which have been recreated on the spot can be seen from 'time-cars' in the popular Jorvik Centre. Despite attempts to rehabilitate the Vikings as peaceful artisans their bloodthirsty image still lingers. After all Eric Bloodaxe did rule here. . .

Middle Ages

York was one of England's richest and most important trading cities — more than 100 crafts flourished here — each with its own strict trade union or guild. Merchants built themselves fine halls such as the Merchant Adventurers and the Merchant Tailors. Some of the guilds have been reformed and their members wine and dine their guests by candlelight under oak raftered ceilings.

The walls around York are medieval and so is much of the narrow street pattern. Medieval monarchy were frequent visitors — Henry III's sister and daughter were both married in the Minster. The title of Duke of York for the monarch's second son was another mark of the city's importance.

More grimly during the medieval wars heads were displayed on the gateways — a Duke of York's head once looked down on 'his' city from Micklegate Bar. The Middle Ages have also left a strong literary legacy — the York Mystery plays — originally performed on wagons by the guilds in the city streets and revived as part of the periodic York Festivals which began in 1951.

Civil War

Charles I stayed in York for a time and minted money in the city while waging a propaganda war on the Parliamentarians from his printing press in St. William's College. When the Parliamentarians besieged the city in 1644 mines were exploded under the walls at St. Mary's Tower. Walmgate Bar still shows the scars of cannon balls. Forced to surrender after the Royalist disaster at Marston Moor the city probably owes the success of its tourism industry to a Parliamentarian, Sir Thomas Fairfax. The

York Minster from the city walls   Clifford Robinson

Roundheads could have laid waste to the city but Sir Thomas, a Yorkshireman, was a model of restraint as Governor and the city survived with its future tourist attractions still intact.

Georgian Times

An age of elegant town houses as York became the social centre for the northern aristocracy providing them not only with homes, but meeting rooms, a race course, hospitals, prisons and court buildings.

Their homes, now converted into offices, schools or shops, can be seen in Micklegate and Bootham while Fairfax House in Castlegate has been refurbished in Georgian style. The Assembly Rooms where lavish balls and banquets were held in the 18th century has become, after many vicissitudes, a tea room. The Georgian Female and Debtors' Prison have become a Museum but the Georgians' grand Assize Courts remain as courts.

Victorian Times

"Mak' all t'railways cum to York", said George Hudson, York's Railway 'king'. Nevertheless they removed his portrait from the Mansion House when he was caught fiddling his railway company books. But it was George's railways which brought prosperity to York expanding small shop based firms like Rowntree's and Terry's into major industries and encouraging the erection of new public buildings, churches, college and town houses.

The best things in York are free...

It is possible to visit York and spend absolutely nothing at all...

York Minster: The city's biggest and best tourist attraction. Entrance is free if your conscience lets you ignore the prominently displayed collection boxes. (See Minster section for details.)

Guided walks: No charge is made by the Association of Voluntary Guides whose tours start from Exhibition Square every summer morning and afternoon. Details from the Tourist Information office, Exhibition Square (01904 621756).

With a good map (again from the Information Office) you can make up your own tours.

The City Walls: Some three miles of medieval fortifications encircling nearly the whole city. The best section runs from Bootham Bar to Monk Bar with views of the Minster, pantiled roof tops and the back gardens of grand town houses. At Monk Bar the 'sentries' are still on guard, carved figures frozen in the act of dropping boulders on attackers.

Another good section runs from Micklegate Bar, where traitors' heads were once displayed, past the railway station to the famous view of the city along the walls to the minster before dropping down to the river at Barker Tower. (The information office has a detailed wall walk map).

The Streets: A history lesson free for the looking. If

possible look above the goods on display in the shop fronts and appreciate the architecture above. Everywhere is half timbered medieval, Georgian elegance and proportion and Victorian ornamentation.

The Shambles: Where the half timbered houses lean to within handshaking distance of each other is probably one of the best preserved medieval streets in Europe. St. Margaret of York lived at No. 35. The medieval butchers have given way to tea, souvenir and craft shops. The medieval atmosphere still clings but mercifully not the medieval smells.

Stonegate: Once the main road of Roman York and now an elegant pedestrianised street and home for fine art shops and boutiques. For more plain tastes an ancient ale house, Ye Olde Starre Inne, can be reached down an alleyway.

High Petergate and Petergate: The main city cross road in Roman times which begins squeezed behind Bootham Bar and suddenly reveals the height and

Guildhall and the Ouse   *Clifford Robinson*

power of the Minster's West Front before diving back among the old buildings and ending up in King's Square.

Goodramgate: Contains the oldest row of cottages in York — the 14th century Lady Row — and a number of other fine medieval buildings. For good measure it also has a dubious example of 20th century 'commercial redevelopment' — a set of concrete and brick arcaded shop fronts. It so stunned and annoyed conservationists that planners were pressured into keeping stricter control over what could be erected in the 'historic core'. It remains a good example of what might have been...

College Street, Ogleforth and Chapter House Street: A cluster of quaint cobbled streets behind the Minster which quietly preserve the intimate atmosphere of York's sleepier days.

Micklegate: The grand entrance to York via Micklegate Bar end lined with fine Georgian houses. Joseph Hansom, who invented the Hansom cab lived at number 114. Travelling into the city this way one passes three churches, Holy Trinity, with its stocks still

Micklegate   *Stanley Bond*

ready at the gate, St. Martin cum Gregory further down the hill and St. John the Evangelist, now converted into a lively Arts Centre.

Entertainment: Can be found all over the city centre — free. On fine days buskers are on nearly every corner with the repetition of favourite tunes often driving the nearest shopkeepers to distraction. The main 'stage' is in King's Square where al fresco fish and chips on a bench comes with fire eaters and jugglers on the side. Still more entertainers can be found in slightly more sedate surroundings in Parliament Street which is rapidly acquiring a continental look with its trees, fountain and pavement chess and draughts.

Culture: The city Art Gallery is free and welcomes young visitors with 'picture spotting' sheets so children can hunt out the Old Masters. Lectures and recitals as well as painting sessions and craft workshops take place during school holidays. Check the gallery bulletin board for details (01904 623839). (See also entertainments section.)

Picnics and some peace and quiet: The Museum Gardens — 10 acres of trees and lawns with a ruined abbey and an old Roman tower providing a romantic backdrop.

York Minster

The Minster is the largest, medieval Gothic church in England. The 'basement' stands on the massive remains of a Roman fortress and the Central Tower roof gives magnificent views across the city — but only after a breathless climb up 279 spiralling stone steps. Information leaflets available inside cover every possible aspect of this religious, historical treasure house. Pick one up on whatever subject interests you and browse. . .

At ground level there is a world of stained glass artistry, ornate tombs, intricate carving, tranquil chapels and the superb new ceiling in the south transept restored after the 1984 fire.

Don't dismiss the 'basement' area as potentially

boring. Here the cathedral's modern, steel reinforced concrete 'feet' lie side by side with earlier building work by Romans and Normans — 2,000 years of history piled on top of itself.

Although many of the 2,250,000 visitors a year are looking only for architecture and history, this is a living church and when the sounds of chorister and organ momentarily still the constant shuffling of visitors' feet, the minster takes on a more profound purpose.

The minster has its own visitors' centre in nearby St. William's College with exhibitions of cathedral life down the ages. The Minster Close is worth exploring: half timbered St. William's College, Gray's Court with its cobbled courtyard and plane trees and Treasurer's House, a NT 17th/18th century town house with fine rooms and furniture, a secluded garden and reputedly a ghostly Roman legion tramping through its cellars.

Treasurers House: Opening times: 26 March-30 October, every day 10.30-5. Administrator (01904 624247) for details of special events and evening opening. Admission charges: Adults £3; children free during school holidays at other times £1.75. Trust members free.

The Minster Library in Dean's Park (01904 625308) formerly a 13th century chapel, is the largest cathedral library in the country.

The minster is open 7-8.30 in summer; 7-5 in winter. Charges are made for some other areas.

Other Churches: Holy Trinity, Goodramgate, built between 1250 and 1500 with cosy 18th century box pews and intriguing gravestones in the floor.

Reached through an easily-missed iron gate in Goodramgate it has a forgotten timeless quality.

All Saints, Pavement. In darker days a lantern used to shine from the octagonal tower to guide travellers to York. The doom knocker shows what happened to them if they misbehaved — they are swallowed by a devil at the mouth of hell. The City Guilds process to their services here and their symbols are displayed on the walls. All Saints, North Street. Famous for its 15th century stained glass and carved ceiling.

St. Martin-le-Grand, Coney Street. The 15th century church had its stained glass scattered into the molten tar of the main street when it was firebombed in 1942. The ruins have been turned into a paved garden as a shrine for those lost in two world wars.

Oglethorpe   *Clifford Robinson*

Museums

National Rail Museum: The sheer size of this museum never fails to impress — two vast halls full of mechanical steam monsters — the beautiful and the downright ugly. Evocative sounds of shunting, and the clattering of trains over the points drift in the air to add to the nostalgia. Everything is here that the railway buff could possibly want to see. Little boys of all ages can climb into many of the locomotives and play train drivers.

Opening times: Monday to Saturday 10-6, Sunday 11-6. Closed Christmas Eve, Christmas Day, Boxing Day and New Year's Day. Admission charges: Adult £4.20, child £2.10, senior citizens and concessions £2.80 (01904 621261).

York Castle Museum: Deservedly popular museum of everyday life and possibly, after the Rail Museum, the best value for money in the city. Hours can be spent exploring the reconstructed Victorian streets and shops and the period rooms with 'antique' everyday items up to the 1950s.

The collections fill the former Female and Debtors' Prison — historic and fascinating buildings in their own right. The cell where Dick Turpin spent his last night is here and the court where he was sentenced is next door. Other cells with their grim bars and bolts now contain craft workshops. Relics of Yorkshire battles, militaria, costume and accessories and children's toys fill the other galleries. A few attendants dressed as helpful Victorian 'bobbies' or prison warders would, however, make a fine museum even finer.

Opening times: 9.30-5.30; Sundays 10-5.30. Closed Christmas and Boxing Days and New Year's Day. Admission charges: Adults £3.95; children, stu-

Fishermen on the River Foss, as depicted at the Jorvic Viking Centre

dents and senior citizens £2.85 (01904 653611).

Jorvik Viking Centre: Public fascination with the old rapers and pillagers still keeps the customers piling into the time-cars to shuttle through these underground fibreglass streets of 10th century Viking York. In high season the staff put notice-boards alongside the huge queues: 'One hour wait from here ...' so avoid school holidays! That famous time-car journey lasts only 15 minutes and the rest of the visit is taken up with display cases and a well filled souvenir shop. Memories of a trip through noisy, smelly old Jorvik, however, will probably stay with youngsters for a lifetime. Academic noses may have been turned up at the whole concept and sniffy mutterings made about a Viking Disneyland but at the popular level this is history brought imaginatively to life.

Opening times: 1 April to 31 October 9-7, 1 November to 31 March 9-5.30. Admission charges: Adults £3.95, under 16 £2, senior citizens £3. Children under five free. Winter reductions for York residents: Adults £2, children £1 (01904 643211).

Yorkshire Museum: The permanent displays represent Roman, Anglo Saxon and Viking times with a section recreating life in St. Mary's Abbey, part of whose ruins lie under the museum. There is also a piece of jewellery which cost the museum £2.5m — a 15th century gold pendant set with a sapphire, found at Middleham Castle in 1985. Imaginative touring exhibitions — everything from dinosaurs to Vikings have been on offer — are regularly staged.

Opening times: 10-5 every day (November to March) Sunday opening 1-5. Closed Christmas and Boxing Days and New Year's Day. Admission charges: Adults £3, senior citizens and students £1.75, children under five free (01904 629745).

City Art Gallery: Seven centuries of art, continental and British and including the Lycett Green collection of Old Masters. Local born William Etty's works are on display and a collection of stoneware pottery donated by a former Dean of York, the Very Rev. E. Milner-White. See the gallery notice board for a changing programme of temporary exhibitions, lectures and other events.

Opening times: Monday to Saturday 10-5. Sunday 2.30-5. Closed January 1, Good Friday, December 25-26. Admission free (01904 623839).

The ARC (Archaeological Resource Centre), St. Saviourgate, York: This is the place where budding Indiana Joneses can get their hands on some real archaeological finds. Young visitors can sift through trays of 'dig debris' picking out the pottery fragments, re-assembling animal bones, or trying their hands at 'unpicking' Viking locks, spinning and weaving, even making shoes Viking style. Interactive videos allow excavations to be 'explored' layer by layer on the TV screen. It is a clever mixture of 'high tech' and earthy 'hands on' experiences.

Open Monday to Friday 10 to last admission 4.30, Saturday and Sunday 1 to 4.30. Closed Good Friday, 17 to 26 December, 31 December, 1 January. Entrance charges: Adults £3.20, children under 16 £2.10 (01904 654324).

Barley Hall: A refurbished 15th century town house tucked away in Grape Lane in the city centre is another venture by the York Archaeological Trust but they still have a long way to go to repeat the success of their Jorvik Centre. The restored, timber-framed home of Alderman William Snawsell, goldsmith, is being slowly filled with furniture and wall hangings made by modern craftsmen in medieval ways. But as yet it looks a little bare and lacks atmosphere.

Opening times: Monday to Saturday 10-4.30 (closed Sundays). Closed Good Friday and between December 20 and January 4. Adults £3, children £2 (01904 652398).

Fairfax House: If Lord Fairfax could walk back into his Georgian town house in Castlegate he would find it much the same as he left it in the 18th century. Rescued from decay by the York Civic Trust and housing the Terry collection of furniture it has become one of the finest 18th century townhouses in England. Despite an aura of elegance it is still a 'living' building often used for small private banquets and dinner parties, when candles flicker on silver and polished mahogany.

Opening times 11-5, 1 March to 31 December, Sundays 1.30-5 (closed Fridays). Admission charges £3 adults, £2.50 senior citizens, £1.50 children. 'Keeping of Christmas' exhibition, December 3 to January 6 (excluding Fridays, Christmas Day and Boxing Day). Connoisseur Tours and private parties by arrangement (01904 655543).

Museum of Automata: The clowns in their end-of-the-pier glass cases and all those mechanical acrobats and dancers are very clever but they look a bit sad and pointless these days. One is uncomfortably aware that their successors — the electronic factory robots — are no longer so naive. They are, after all, starting to take over...

Open every day except Christmas Day. 9.30-5.30 (January 10-4). Admission: Adults £3.20, children £1.95, senior citizens/students £2.80 (01904 655550).

York Story: The city fathers found a good use for the redundant St. Mary's Church in Castlegate — they turned it into a heritage centre. Models, drawings, paintings and an audio visual presentation give visitors a quick gallop through 1,000 years of the

The Hospitium, St. Mary's Abbey   *F. L. Jackson*

city's history and architecture. A useful starting point for a visit to the city. Admission times: 10-5, Sunday 1-5. Closed Christmas and Boxing Days and New Year's Day. Admission charges: Adults £1.50, senior citizens, children £1. (01904 628632).

Friargate Museum: A waxworks museum with a collection of Royalty, past and present, the famous and infamous, and some of those of more fleeting fame making a brief appearance before going back into the melting pot ready for the next 'personality' to rise. Currently the museum is re-creating the atmosphere of war time London and the Blitz. Opening times: From mid January to end of November, every day 10-5. Entrance charges: Adults £2.50, senior citizens £2, children £1.50 (01904 658775).

The York Dungeon: If your idea of a holiday outing is to feel stunned, shocked and depressed at man's inhumanity to man or if your personal nightmares are running out of ideas then this is the place for you. Blood, gore, moans and groans ... "Whatever melts your butter", as the Americans say. Opening times: April to October, every day 10-5.30 (closes 4.30 at other times). Shut Christmas Day. Admission charges £3.25, children and senior citizens £2, students £2.75 (01904 632599).

Historic Buildings

Assembly Rooms: Grandeur has returned to this Georgian idea of an Egyptian temple with its re-use as a tearoom. Built in the 1730s it was once the centre of York's social life and the venue for great balls and assemblies. Now there are genteel cakes and tea served between the marbled pillars.

Clifford's Tower: William the Conqueror is said to have thrown up this tower mound in just a month and put a wooden castle on top. A century later some 150 Jews trapped inside took their lives rather than submit to a howling city mob. On Guy Fawkes Night the present 13th century stone tower is the setting for an impressive free fireworks display. Good views from the parapet. Information panels inside tell the castle's story. Opening times: Good Friday (or 1 April whichever is earlier) to 31 October, daily 10-6. 1 November to Maundy Thursday (or 31 March whichever is earlier), daily 10 to 4. Closed 24 to 26 December and January 1. (01904 646940). Admission charges: Adults £1.50, concessions £1.10, children 75p.

Crown Courts: Built in the 18th century and complementing the nearby female and debtors' prisons built in the same Georgian style. Grass arena in front of the courts is called the Eye of York and popular for picnics with school parties.

Guildhall: Where the city fathers meet in their carved Victorian council chamber. Cash to the Scots for the capture of Charles I was counted out in one of the committee rooms and there are secret doorways in the panelling. The common hall was destroyed in a German bombing raid in 1942. Later restored it is used for meetings and exhibitions.

King's Manor: An imposing group of buildings entered through an ancient gateway topped by a magnificent coat of arms. As the name implies, James I and Charles I stayed here, although originally it was the home of the Abbot of St. Mary's. Now part of York University. Admission free.

Mansion House: The home for a year of the Lord Mayor of York and his Lady. Attractive Georgian facade with a doll's house quality particularly when flower decked and floodlit. Visits can be arranged through the Civic Secretary, Mansion House, York (01904 613161).

Merchant Adventurers' Hall: The largest timber framed building in the city which comes alive by candlelight for dinners and social occasions. From here the once powerful merchant adventurers' guild expanded trade and maintained craft standards or, according to political viewpoint, operated the country's first closed shop. Open seven days a week 8.30-5. Closed Christmas week and on winter Sundays, early November to late March. Admission: Adults

£1.80, senior citizens and students £1.50, children 50p (01904 654818).

Merchant Tailors' Hall: The home of another once powerful guild. Panelled walls and a 14th century timbered room. Open Mondays only 10-4 from Easter until 1 October. no charge (01904 624889).

St. Anthony's Hall: Its guild was dissolved in the 17th century. As part of York University it now houses the Borthwick Institute for Historical Research and a vast collection of diocesan records. Appointments necessary to consult the archives (01904 642315).

St. Leonard's Hospital: (Close to the City Library.) The ruined leftovers of a former medieval hospital. Free admission.

St. Mary's Abbey: A romantic ruin in the Museum Gardens which has made an impressive backcloth for modern productions of the city's medieval Mystery Plays during York Festivals. The St. Mary's monastery complex once covered this whole area but only small sections survive. The hospitium where the Abbot entertained is now a museum and the gatehouse has become the Marygate entrance to the Gardens.

Black Swan Inn, Peasholme Green: Once the home of Martin Bowes, goldsmith to Queen Elizabeth and twice Lord Mayor of London. Panelled rooms and cheery fires in winter. Open usual public house hours (01904 624481).

Roman Bath Inn, St. Samson's Square: Busy city centre public house. Glass 'window' in the floor shows the remains of the heating area and ducting for the Roman garrison's steam baths (01904 620455).

Entertainment

Theatre Royal, St. Leonard's Place: Everything from the classics to musicals on offer according to season (01904 623568).

Grand Opera House, Clifford Street: Former music hall now staging touring company productions (01904 671818).

Barbican Centre, Barbican Road: Modern theatre

Merchant Adventurers Hall   *Clifford Robinson*

complex, comedy and concerts (01904 670977).

Arts Centre, Micklegate: Former church converted into an intimate venue for poetry, drama and films (01904 627129).

City Art Gallery, Exhibition Square: Lunchtime entertainments on alternate Tuesdays throughout the year (01904 623839).

University of York, Heslington: Orchestral concerts and recitals. Also the York Film Theatre (01904 430000).

York Leisure Services: Organises concerts, light entertainment and sporting events (01904 613161).

Cinemas: Warner Bros, Clifton Moor Estate (01904 691094). York Odeon, Blossom Street (10904 623040). York City Screen, Museum Gardens (01904 612940).

Information

There are Tourist Information Centres at Exhibition Square (01904 621756), the Railway Station (01904 643700) and at the Travel Offices, Rougier Street (01904 620557).

Accommodation: Where to stay guides available at above.

Car parking: A nightmare unless thought about in advance. Park and Ride recommended for most stays. Facilities at Tadcaster Road and on the Clifton Moor Estate, signposted on approaches to city: charges from 80p. Short stay multi-storey car parks at Shambles, Piccadilly and Foss Bank (all signposted) starting at 40p an hour and rising to about £3.50 for five hours.

Shopping: The city is devoted to it — expensive porcelain and silver in places like Stonegate, bric-a-brac in the market, antiques, exclusive boutiques, small craft shops and multiple stores. Every day (except Sunday) is Market Day.

Eating out: A bewildering choice — everything from ancient public houses to elegant restaurants and tea rooms, bistros and wine bars. Wander the city centre and take your pick.

Sport: Soccer, York City FC at Bootham Crescent (01904 62447). Cricket and Rugby Union, Clifton Park (01904 623602). Rugby League, Jockey Lane, Huntington (01904 634636). Racing, Knavesmire: Five race meetings a year (01904 620911). Golf: Fulford (01904 412882. York Golf Club, Strensall (01904 491840). Heworth (01904 424618) and Pike Hills (01904 706566).

2 NORTH YORK MOORS

by Harry Mead

On the drive across Kildale Moor to Westerdale, a magnificent spectacle opens out. Immediately ahead, amid bracken and heather, the road plunges to the wild valley of Baysdale Beck. Beyond, a series of interlocking moorland ridges form a Cinemascope panorama. Trailing along some of the ridges are the narrow roads characteristic of the area. The most prominent, a bright thread when sunshine follows rain, rises out of Westerdale and aims for a horizon of still higher moors — the loftiest ground in the national park.

Here is the spirit of the North York Moors. The lungs expand at the prospect of so much fresh air. The feet itch to tramp those ridges and discover the valleys

2 NORTH YORK MOORS

WHITBY
STOKESLEY
GOATHLAND
OSMOTHERLEY
KIRKBYMOORSIDE
SCARBOROUGH
PICKERING
HELMSLEY
THIRSK
MALTON

they so sharply define. There is an uplifting sense of freedom and space.

Yet oddly, these moors are not those commonly perceived as the 'Yorkshire Moors'. Intimately associated with the Brontes, those other moors are a sombre link in the Pennine chain, some 60 miles away. And although on a bad day the North York Moors could easily stand in as a harsh and desolate setting for Wuthering Heights, they generally show little of the bleakness of their Bronte counterparts.

At their heart, of course, is the famous expanse of heather, the largest in England and Wales, that was the principal reason they were designated a National

Helmsley Castle   *Derek Widdicombe*

Park in 1952. Covering about 30pc of the park, the heather cloaks the moor tops for almost 40 miles — from the Vale of York to the North Sea. In late summer its myriad of tiny flowers, calculated by one botanist to bloom at a density of 3,000 million per square mile, turns the brown moorland carpet into a foaming, upland purple sea.

Green fields are never far away. For pastoral dales, smaller than most in the Dales National Park, finger their way into the highest moors. Even in the most apparently remote spot, a walker is never far from at least one, and often more, of these homely valleys. Their field boundaries are as likely to be hedges — hawthorn, alder and rowan — as stone walls. And under their russet pantiles their farmhouses and cottages are built of either honey-coloured sandstone or creamy limestone — a marked contrast to the grey slates and dark millstone grit of the Bronte Moors. Tucked away in one or two places, like Rievaulx and Pockley, are thatched cottages as snug as any in Suffolk.

Not all the national park, 553 square miles in all, is moorland or upland dale. The coast is the most obvious non-moorland element. Hardly less so are the commercial forests, which occupy about 20pc of the park. Once hated as ugly and alien, these are being carefully restructured to create less rigid plantations, of a greater variety of trees, in stands of mixed ages. A car drive through the Dalby forest has long been popular, and people now book for walks to hear the nightjar. This is one of several wildlife species, the most notable being roe and fallow deer, that have greatly benefited by the forest. Since plenty of open moor remains, the new generation of forests can perhaps be accepted as a making a positive contribution to the unusually diverse landscapes within the 'Moors'.

The variety gives the walker generous scope to tailor walks to the seasons. The spring pilgrimage to Farndale, bright with its seven famous riverside miles of wild daffodils, is a must for most moorland devotees. But the pageant of spring flowers in the four or five extensive stretches of native woodland in the moors is no less rewarding. The walk through Sinnington Woods to Cropton, with anemones, violets, primroses, cowslips, orchids and other flowers brushing one's boots almost the whole way, is among the loveliest anywhere.

The high moors demand to be visited when the heather is in bloom — August to mid September. The spectacle is only part of the experience. On a windy day, the fragrance is like lifting the lid on a giant pot of honey. But the moors are arguably more impressive — and certainly their truer selves — in winter. Their silence is almost tangible and definitely therapeutic: you can feel it soaking into you.

Most people should find something to interest them here. Archaeology? With literally hundreds of prehistoric earthworks, the Moors are one of the most potent links with some of our earliest ancestors. It is always a thrill to find one of their tiny flints, scraper perhaps or primitive knife blade, knowing you are the first person to handle it for about 5,000 years.

Geologically too the Moors have much to show. In Eskdale and its tributary valleys a glacier from the North Sea created a series of lakes. One overflow channel, the shallow Randy Mere, near Goathland, became a gathering ground for medical leeches. Another, the canyon-like Newton Dale, was adopted by George Stephenson as the route of the Whitby-Pickering Railway. It still echoes with steam trains, operated by the North Yorkshire Moors Railway.

The site of Rievaulx Abbey, perhaps Britain's most sublime ruin, was described as "a place of horror" by its founding monks in 1131. The changes they wrought were mirrored in a description penned by the third abbot, Aelred: "Everywhere peace, everywhere serenity and a marvellous freedom from the tumult of the world." This is now often applied to the Moors as a whole.

And yet there's scarcely any corner of the Moors

White Horse of Kilburn from the village
John Edenbrow

that hasn't been hacked and wrenched. At Rievaulx itself, in 1577, shortly after the abbey was dissolved, the North's first blast-furnace arose. Some of its clinker can still be found in Ashberry Wood. In Rosedale, towering ruined kilns tell of the valley's epic Victorian days as ironstone-mining Klondyke.

The bent summit of Roseberry Topping, the region's most eye-catching peak, is a legacy of quarrying. Elsewhere, the working of jet, coal and alum, the latter sometimes described as the first chemical industry, have all left distinctive marks on the landscape.

The heather itself emerged as the woods that once clothed the region were cut down from the Bronze Age onwards. Since Victorian times it has been expertly managed to sustain grouse shooting — the main economic activity of the high moors, with sheep farming as runner up.

From mid winter to spring sulphurous columns of smoke signal "burning off". Carried out over a 15-year cycle on each moor, this controlled firing of the heather creates a patchwork in which the grouse can find food (fresh heather shoots), nesting sites (young heather) and shelter (older heather).

The red grouse, object of all this attention, is only found here in Britain. As winter ends it is joined on its moorland stronghold by other familiar upland species — snipe, curlew, plover. Particularly worth watching for is the merlin, Britain's smallest bird of prey, fond of perching on clumps of heather.

Occasionally there is also the magnificent spectacle of a hunting hen harrier: a bird of huge wing span, it flies low and slowly over the moors, suddenly veering sideways to catch its prey. The moors near Scaling Dam, and Fylingdales, appear to be its strongholds.

For visitors who enjoy just pottering, popular villages like Lealholm and Hutton-le-Hole, and the market towns on the fringe, provide plenty to see and do. And anyone exploring largely by car need not fear that the Kildale-Westerdale road is the only one that reveals the majesty of the moors.

The route from Egton Bridge to Rosedale, crossing a moor where local people still cut peat, and the journey between Osmotherley and Hawnby, through Snilesworth, the loneliest inhabited part of the Moors, are no less memorable.

If extended to the top of Newgate Bank, on the Helmsley-Stokesley road, the Snilesworth drive captures perhaps the finest prize of all. For the bird's eye view of Bilsdale, revealing the cheerful chequerwork of fields and little woods running up to the expansive moor is perhaps more than just the essence of the

North York Moors. Some would say it is the essence of England.

North York Moors in detail

ABBREVIATIONS: EH — English Heritage. NT — National Trust. Entries are grouped in districts based on the principal towns. Beginning at Whitby, these proceed round the moors in an anti-clockwise direction. Where a mileage is given, this means from that town.

WHITBY AREA

Goathland: 7m south off A169 Pickering road. A long-time moorland favourite, this invigorating village has gained extra fame as the setting of TV's Heartbeat series, based on the adventures of a village constable. Most of the village dates only from the arrival of the Whitby-Pickering railway in the 1860s. Where the moor rises to the south, the former bunkers and greens of a golf course created for early visitors but abandoned during the Second World War can still be discerned.

A nearby glacial overflow channel was dammed to form a skating pond, named on maps as The Tarn, for guests at the Mallyan Spout Hotel. A bus shelter is gated against the village's ubiquitous sheep, which will enter picnickers' cars if allowed to. Of several local waterfalls, the lace-curtain Mallyan Spout, often little more than a thread, is the best known, but Water Ark, in a suntrap bowl with seats, is the most attractive. A well preserved section of Roman Road runs on Wheeldale Moor, and the 1894 church, by Walter Brierley of York (the "Lutyens of the North") contains an ancient stone altar that might have come from a 12th century hermitage — the beginning of Goathland.

Beck Hole: 1m from Goathland. The view into this hamlet as you enter down a steep hill from Grosmont is like peering into fairyland. Beyond the chimney pots and rooftops of cottages almost directly below

Goathland   *D. Mark Thompson*

stand more cottages in an arc facing a little raised green. Quoits, a game popular throughout the Whitby district, here has its most picturesque setting. Odd-looking boxes on the green are covers for the clay pitches, and photographs of quoits' teams hang at the bar of the unspoilt Birch Hall Inn. Fixed to its outside wall is an oil painting by Sir Algernon Newton, a noted Victorian artist, who lived in the village. Three contrasting paths to Goathland — riverside, old railway incline, and a turfy moor enfolding the green hollow of Darnholme — give a matchless choice of lovely half-day walks.

Fylingdales: 9m south by A169 Pickering road. In 1993 a so-called "pyramid" replaced the much-admired 'golf balls' radar domes erected in 1963 to warn of nuclear attack. The new structure serves the same purpose but lacks the golf balls' eerie rapport with the moors. Certain to outlast the new arrival is the 7th century Lilla Cross, on nearby Lilla Howe. Believed to mark the grave of Lilla, a servant of King

Edwin, who died saving the King from an assassin's dagger, it is regarded as the oldest Christian monument in the North.

ESKDALE

Yorkshire's only salmon river, the Esk runs for about 30 miles from Esklets, at the head of Westerdale, to the sea at Whitby. Fed by several tributary valleys, Eskdale is the broadest and longest valley in the moors and the only one running west to east. A 35-mile national park trail, the Esk Valley Walk, follows its course from source to mouth. A valley road links its numerous villages, most of which can also be reached off the A171 Guisborough road. The dale is also well seen from the highly scenic Esk Valley (Middlesbrough-Whitby) railway. From east to west its places of interest include:

Grosmont: Northern terminus of the North Yorkshire Moors Railway, the preserved line that runs 18 miles to Pickering. The castellated tunnel used by the original horse-drawn trains leads to loco sheds open to the public. An attractive walk follows an abandoned section of the original line to Goathland, via Beck Hole. The walk to Whitby, following a trod that linked Whitby Abbey with the vanished Grosmont Priory, is also worthwhile.

Egton Bridge: Big trees and a sylvan stretch of river make this the most romantic of the Esk villages. Two sets of stepping stones cross the river where it splits to encircle a small island, on which Victorian picnics were held. In St. Hedda's Roman Catholic church is a shrine to a martyred 17th century local Roman Catholic priest, Nicholas Postgate. He celebrated Mass in a secret room in a house ever since called The Mass House. As its date stone reveals, the village's beautiful bridge was built only in 1993. It is an exact replica, on stronger foundations, of a medieval bridge swept away in a flood of 1930 and replaced by an ugly iron structure.

Gooseberry Show: Berries almost the size of golf balls are the order of the day at this rare show, one of only two or three in Britain devoted exclusively to the humble goosegog. Tiny weights, some no more than thin slivers of metal, are used to gauge the weight of each berry, expressed in drams and grains. Tipping the scales at 30 drams 8 grains, almost 2oz, a berry shown in 1952 held the world record for 30 years.

Agricultural show: Wednesday before August bank holiday.

Glaisdale: Ironworks once dominated this scattered Eskdale village. The former view from The Angler's Rest was reflected in the pub's original name — The Three Blast-furnaces. Nearby Beggar's Bridge was built in 1619 by Tom Ferres, whose initials are on the parapet. In love with the squire's daughter he was told she couldn't marry a beggar. A flood prevented him crossing a ford to see his sweetheart before he set out to make his fortune. Returning rich — the fruit of piracy, say some — he built the bridge so that the river would never again keep lovers apart.

Lealholm: A riverside green, stepping stones, and a pub overlooking an anglers' pool contribute to making this the most popular Esk Valley village. Much of its character is due to Sir Francis Ley, a Nottingham industrialist who owned the village early this century and planted trees, built model cottages and installed three drinking fountains, whose canopied covers still survive. Poet's Cottage, a thriving shrub nursery, was the home of an 18th century dialect poet and mason John Castillo. The chapel wall bears flood markers, and a plaque on a boulder at Lealholmside, up the hill towards the Whitby road, commemorates two US airmen who died when their jet fighter bomber crashed there in 1979, narrowly missing the village school.

Danby: The remains of 14th century Danby Castle, home of Catherine Parr, the last of Henry VIII's six wives, are absorbed into a farmhouse where, each autumn, a manor court, administering moor rights, still sits.

The six farms at the head of Danby Dale form the Botton Community, where 300 people, mentally-handicapped and co-workers, live and work together on the land and in variety of craft shops. Visitors are welcome and an annual open day is held in July. 01287 660871.

Restored watermill near village station: Easter-November, Wed-Sun, 10.30-5.30. £1, children and others 50p.

The Moors Centre, Danby Lodge: The main national park information centre, with exhibitions and waymarked walks. April-October daily, 10-5; Nov-March weekends, 11-4. Free. 01287 660654

Agricultural Show: Wednesday in mid August.

Westerdale: Literally the most westerly of the main dales traditionally linked to Whitby. In Westerdale what looks like a fortified manor house was the Victorian shooting lodge of the Earl of Feversham. A medieval cross that stood near the junction of the Castleton road was destroyed last century by a farmer angry that it had caused his cart to overturn. Through the garden gate of the village's most southerly cottage can be seen the Bulmer Stone, a pillar on a large plinth, carved with a wordy inscription recounting the sea voyages and shipwrecks of mariner Thomas Bulmer, who lived in the cottage. Hob Hole, a oasis of sheep-cropped turf by a watersplash on the road to Kildale, is a popular picnic spot.

Commondale: A village of harsh red brick, a legacy of a former brickyard. A stone cross by the track to Guisborough stands where two local shepherd lads, killed in the First World War, used to meet while gathering their flocks. Members and veterans of their former regiment trek there to pay homage every sum-

Delves Cottage near Egton Bridge   *Den Oldroyd*

mer.

Baysdale: As a punishment for slack behaviour, a Cistercian nunnery was transferred in the 12th century from the Vale of Cleveland to this remote valley, with only a single road in and out. But the nuns remained unruly, and one group, headed by the prioress, ran away. Only the high-arched bridge that led to the priory sur-vives, and the site is now occupied by a farm and shooting lodge, named on the map as Baysdale

Lilla Cross

Abbey. Armouth Wath, the wild dale head, where two streams crossed by little slabbed bridges meet by a ruined sheephouse, is full of the atmosphere of the moors.

Ralph Cross (and others): Surviving in whole or part throughout the moors are about 30 ancient stone crosses. Most were erected as waymarkers, intended to give Christian comfort to people crossing this wilderness. The best known, the emblem of the national park, is Ralph Cross, on the moor road between the Eskdale village of Castleton and Hutton-le-Hole. Properly known as Young Ralph this was put in the 18th century, perhaps to indicate a change in the moor road, although some say it marks where a farmer found a victim of a snowstorm. A distinctive nick in the cross's top is said be where wealthy trav-ellers placed coins, to be collected by more needy passers by.

A more ancient cross, Old Ralph, stands at the junction of three parishes a few hundred yards to the west of Young Ralph, while the whitewashed base and wheelhead of yet another cross, Fat Betty, is along the nearby Rosedale Road. It is said that if Young Ralph and Fat Betty meet there will be wedding — presumably with Old Ralph as principal guest.

STOKESLEY DISTRICT

Stokesley: Pop 3,830. Rising abruptly from the Cleveland Plain four miles away, the dramatic switchback ridge of the Cleveland Hills gives Stokesley the most impressive moorland backdrop of all the market towns serving the region. The town itself, with wide partly-cobbled High Street, three-storey Georgian buildings in old brick, and central town hall, has much charm. An ancient packhorse bridge is among five footbridges that link the town centre with Levenside, a peaceful riverside area.

Market Day: Friday

Agricultural Show: One of the North's biggest one day shows, held on the Thursday preceding the third Saturday in September. It is accompanied by a three-day fair that fills the High St.

Bilsdale: The only valley that carries a North-South road (B1257 Stokesley-Helmsley) through the moors. Legend says the name is the result of William the Conqueror getting lost on the local moors: a Bilsdale figure of speech, "swearing like Billy Norman", is still heard. Park Dyke, a deep furrow running for about five miles along the moor at the head of the valley, is the longest earthwork in the national park — most probably the boundary of a medieval deer park. Villagers at Fangdale Beck are intensely proud of their rare green phone box. In 1993 BT caused outrage by replacing it with a modern type. Chastened by a £3,000 fine BT swiftly reinstated a traditional box — in fresh green paint.

Spout House: An astonishing amount of history and tradition is concentrated on this roadside thatched building and the neighbouring Sun Inn. A good example of a 16th century 'cruck house', built around a series of timber frames, the Spout was also for many years the headquarters of the Bilsdale Hunt, reputedly the oldest in England. By the door of the Sun Inn, built in 1914, stands the headstone of a noted huntsman. Offended by its hunting motifs, the vicar refused to allow it in the churchyard. Owned and run for at least 200 years by the same Bilsdale family, the Ainsleys, the pub is still primarily an unspoilt 'local'. It has its own cricket team, and a stone in the wall at the top of the field, at the back of the pub, is engraved with a set of stumps in memory of a long-serving secretary. Spout House has been renovated by the national park authority and is open for a small charge, Easter-October daily except Thursday, 10-4.

Agricultural Show: Last Saturday in August.

Botton Head: Reached on foot from Clay Bank, on the B1257 Helmsley Road 5m south. At 1,491ft this highest point of the North York Moors is an undistinguished spot, the unemphatic summit of sprawling Urra Moor.

Great Ayton: Pop 4,480. 3m east on A173. One of Yorkshire's best known villages, set beside the River Leven below the Cleveland Hills. Its strong associations with Captain Cook include his former schoolroom, the obelisk-marked site of his parents' cottage, shipped to Australia in 1934, a prominent monument on Easby Hill, and family graves in the churchyard. Suggitt's ice cream is also a big draw, and a cast-iron Victorian urinal has its admirers — and users.

Captain Cook Schoolroom Museum: Daily April-Oct, 2-4.30, plus weekday mornings in August. £1, children and concessions 50p. 01642 722208 or 723556.

TIC High Green car park. Easter-Oct 31, weekdays 10-4; Sat-Sun 1-4. 01642 722835.

Ingleby Incline: Five miles south of Great Ayton, reached on foot from Bank Foot, near Ingleby Greenhow. Like a ruler line drawn on the slope of the moors, this 1 in 5 mile-long incline was the dramatic

Great Ayton *Bernard Fearnley*

means by which wagons on the Rosedale Railway were lowered from, or hauled to, the high moors. The angle at the top was so acute that when locomotives, generally serviced at Rosedale, were lowered for major maintenance, their central wheels had to be removed.

Carlton: 3m west, Off A172. Attractive village among trees. Built in 1896-7, its 14th century style church arose through the efforts of Canon John Latimer Kyle. He generated the enthusiasm to replace a church completed just a few years earlier but which mysteriously burned down. Its vicar was charged with arson but acquitted.

Mount Grace Priory: 10m west off A19. Britain's best preserved Carthusian ruin, tucked at the foot of the Cleveland Hills near Osmotherley. The Carthusians practised solitary devotion, and each of Mount Grace's 21 monks lived in his own 'cell'. In reality this was a five-roomed house, with running water, efficient sewage disposal and a herb garden — conditions better than those enjoyed by most Britons until this century.

A cell and its garden have been fully restored. Herbs are on sale and there is an excellent exhibition.

EH and NT. April-Sept daily 10-6, October-March Wed and Sun 10am 4pm. £2, Child £1, concessions £1.50. 01609 883249.

Osmotherley: 11m west, off A19. A lofty corner-stone of the Hambleton and Cleveland Hills. With its cobbled centre, where three pubs and several shops cluster at a crossroads complete with an ancient cross and stone "barter table", it seems more like a small town than a village.

The cottage-like Methodist church, up a passage that brings the Cleveland Way right into the centre, contains a stool on which John Wesley stood to preach. Thompson's grocery shop has been in the family since 1786 and has changed little since about 1926. As a tourist attraction it competes with the public toilets, kept spotlessly clean by local woman Ann Cation, who puts flowers in the Ladies.

Lady Chapel: Off Rueberry Lane. Restored 16th century Roman Catholic chapel evolved from a monastic cell licensed in 1397, a year before the founding of nearby Mount Grace Priory.

Worship continued during the persecution of Roman Catholics, making the chapel a place of pilgrimage ever since. It is open daily and mass is celebrated there every Saturday afternoon at 3.30.

Shows: Horticultural — first Sat in August. Summer Games, including finish of annual Lyke Wake Walk Race, second Sat in July.

Lyke Wake Walk: 'Lyke' is an old word for corpse. The traditional Cleveland Lyke Wake Dirge, which describes how a dead person's soul makes a terrible journey over a desolate moor, came into farmer Bill Cowley's mind when he pioneered a 42-mile walk across the then largely trackless tops of the moors, from Osmotherley to the coast at Ravenscar, in 1955.

Since then about 150,000 people have completed the trek in the prescribed 24 hours, entitling them to membership of the Lyke Wake Walk Club, whose emblem is a coffin.

The official starting point is now the Sheepwash, a popular picnic place about two miles east of

Osmotherley.

Inquiries to LWW Club, PO BOX 24, Northallerton. FDL6 3HZ.

THIRSK DISTRICT

Thirsk: Pop 3,850. The principal market town of the Hambleton Hills, which form the western part of the moors. Thomas Lord, founder of Lord's cricket ground, was born in Kirkgate. His house now doubles as the local museum and information centre. Across the road is the veterinary surgery where Alf Wight, alias James Herriot, practised. He and his wife were married in the nearby 15th century parish church. With striking stone fretwork along its parapet, this is one of the best examples in North Yorkshire of the Perpendicular style.

Entertainment: Races: For fixtures phone 01845 522276. Cinema. Studio One. Westgate 01845 524751

Market Days: Monday and Saturday. EC: Wednesday.

TIC and museum: Kirkgate, Easter/April-October.

Osmotherley   *Stanley Bond*

Daily 9.30-5; Sun 2-4. 01845 522755.

Sion Hill Hall: Kirby Wiske, 5miles NW, off A167 Northallerton Road. Homely neo-georgian mansion bought by baker Herbert Mawer in 1961 and stocked with a superb collection of antiques. Now run by a trust, attractions include falconry displays and an exhibition of vintage bicycles, prams and handcarts. Open Mother's Day (March)-October 31. Grounds and Falconry Centre Tues-Sun, 10.30-5.30; House Wed-Sun, 12.30-4.30. 01845 587206.

Sutton Bank: By A 170 6m east. Retired Thirsk vet Alf Wight (James Herriot) regards the view from here, across the Vale of York to the Dales, as the finest in England. Wordsworth was also impressed, notably by Lake Gormire, deep in its glacial fold. A waymarked trail passes near it, and in the opposite direction there's an escarpment path to the Kilburn White Horse (see below). The path passes the Yorkshire Gliding Club, where beginners can have a trial lesson or book a short course. 01845 597237.

National Park Information Centre: Its literature includes an inexpensive guidebook to easy family walks around Sutton Bank. Easter-October, daily 10-5; November-March, weekends only 11-4. 01845 597426

Coxwold   *Janet Leyland*

Kilburn: 5m west, off A19. Village of the mouse and the horse. Ecclesiastical and domestic furniture maker Robert Thompson (1876-1955) carved his first mouse on a church rafter when one of his workmates commented that they were all as poor as church mice. The famous symbol continues to appear on every piece of the oak furniture made in workshops founded by Thompson and now run by his grandsons. The hillside white horse, unique in the North, was cut in 1857 by villagers led by schoolmaster John Hodgson. Because the underlying rock is grey and flaky, only endless grooming prevents this white horse becoming a dark horse and slipping away down the unstable bankside.

Mouseman Visitors' Centre: Housed in Thompson's original workshop is an exhibition devoted to him — and his mouse. Craftsmen are also at work.. April-October Tues-Sun, plus Bank Holidays, l0.30-5.30. Small admission charge. 01347 868218.

Oldstead: 6m west off A19. A walk from this sheltered village climbs to the disused Sneverdale Observatory, built to mark the Coronation of Queen Victoria. Extended to Wass and Byland Abbey the walk make a good half-day stroll.

Coxwold: 8m west off A19. Trim village, with Old Hall, almshouses and cottages set behind the verges and cobbles of a sloping street. At the top is a handsome 15th century church, with a striking octagonal tower. Each May a special cyclists' service is held there — a tradition that dates from 1927.

Shandy Hall: A great bent chimney gives an appropriately quirky look to this house in which parson Laurence Sterne wrote his witty and sometimes bawdy books, Tristram Shandy and A Sentimental Journey. All modern sitcom is said to be derived from them. June-September, Wed 2, Sun 2.30. Parties by appointment. £2 child £1. Garden only £1. 01347 868465.

Newburgh Priory: Converted from an Augustinian Priory this 16th century house is still occupied by descendants of its builders. A sealed tomb is said to contain the remains of Oliver Cromwell, linked to the family by marriage. Visitors also pass through an unfinished room, cursed by a maid who died in a fire. Two attempts to finish it have been swiftly followed by the death of a member of the family. Well-stocked water garden. April 3-June 29, Wed and Sun, 2-6. July 3-August 31, grounds only, Wed and Sun 2-6. Parties by arrangement. £3, children £1; grounds only £1.50, children free. 01347 868435.

HELMSLEY DISTRICT

Helmsley: Pop 1,320. From whichever direction it is approached this main gateway to the national park looks the perfect picture of a small English country town. The shattered castle-keep and pinnacled church tower rise above limestone cottages cradled at the foot of gentle hills, Some cottages face a sparkling beck, and a host of shops and good pubs are grouped round a lively square. Helmsley has the look, and relaxed feel, of the Cotswolds.

The Black Swan is reputedly where William Wordsworth and his sister Dorothy stayed on their way to William's wedding at Brompton. High tea at the Crown is a North Yorkshire institution. The three mile walk to Rievaulx, the first leg of the Cleveland Way, initially gives good views of the town and later, at Griff, commands a fine view of the wooded Rye valley.

Castle: The ruined keep and a well-preserved Tudor Hall are its chief architectural features. In late spring the walls display the blue flowers of the tiny fairy foxglove, an alpine plant sown here by a botanist in the 1930s. EH. April-September, daily 10-6; October-March, Wed-Sun 10-4. £1.80, child 90p concessions £1.35. 01439 770442

Duncombe Park: Present-day Yorkshire craftsman-ship is a feature of this classical mansion, the home of Lord Feversham, who restored it to family use in 1983 after it had been a girls' school for most of this century. The extensive grounds can be visited separately and include circular walks through woodland and by the river. For opening times and prices phone house 01439 770213 or Helmsley TIC, 01439 770173. TIC Market Square March-Oct daily 9.30-6; Nov-Feb weekends. 01439 770173

Rievaulx: 3m north off B1257 Stokesley road. The ruined abbey soars over snug cottages, some thatched, against a backdrop of woods clothing the steep Rye valley: the Moors at their least Moorish. The abbey site was so restricted that the church is aligned North-South. Stone was floated in on barges, along what is believed to have been Britain's first canal, linked to the River Rye. Part of its shallow marshy bed runs alongside a half-mile footpath north to Bow Bridge. Beyond the bridge, a slanting path through Ashberry Wood is the key to an always lovely two-mile circular walk, with high-level views of the abbey through a lacework of trees.

Abbey: Founded in 1131. At its 13th century peak it housed a community of 150 monks and at least 500 lay brothers. EH. April-September, daily 10-6, October-March daily 10-4, £2.20, children £1.10, concessions £1.65. 01439 798228

Rievaulx Abbey   *Geoffrey Wright*

Terrace and Temples: To obtain romantic views of the abbey, an 18th century Helmsley squire, Thomas Duncombe, created a half-mile long curving terrace on the hillside, with a temple at each end and 12 vistas through the trees. Today's visitors can picnic as well as walk on the terrace. One temple is furnished and houses an exhibition. A battery-powered vehicle is available for disabled visitors. NT. March 26-October, daily 10.30-6, £2.50, child £1. 01439 7983406 340.

Byland Abbey

Hawnby: 6m north Off B1257 Stokesley road. With the exceptionally wild moorland of Snilesworth at its back, Hawnby gazes across the gentler landscape of pastures and woods rolling to Rievaulx. The village itself is strangely split — one half, with the pub, at the top of a steep bank, the other, with the shop and PO, at the bottom. Equally striking is the location of nearby Arden Hall, a substantial and lovely country house, in a tight dale head where a rough road begins its climb of the broad-backed hill, Black Hambledon. Dating mainly from the 17th century but incorporating parts of an 11th century priory, the hall is the home of the Earl and Countess of Mexborough and is noted for its huge and billowing yew hedge, seen from the road.

Bransdale: Signposted 'Carlton', the road at the east end of Helmsley continues in a 15-mile loop around Bransdale, emerging at Fadmoor, near Kirkbymoorside. Missed by most motorists it offers those who find it somewhere peaceful to picnic amid magnificent moor scenery. Subject of a poem by John Betjeman, the Victorian church at East Moors, beyond Carlton, is a particularly pleasing moorland church — simple and dignified.

Snowbound curates from Helmsley sometimes slept in hammocks slung across its narrow south aisle, designed to be shuttered off to form a schoolroom. In Bonfield Ghyll a ruined stone aqueduct is part of a complex system of watercourses engineered by a local man, Joe Ford, to supply several 'dry' hilltop villages. Ford apparently made water flow uphill! The theodolite by which he achieved this miracle, and a map of his network, are displayed in Ryedale Folk Museum at Hutton-le-Hole.

Nunnington: 5m south-east off B1257 Malton road. A peaceful village on the slope of Caulkleys Bank, a rare ridge south of the Moors. A path along the ridge descends to Ness, from where a field and riverside path, leads back to Nunnington. Good pub — the Royal Oak.

Nunnington Hall: Appealing small 17th century manor house. Seen from the arched bridge over the Rye, beyond a wide trout pool swept by the branches of a leaning willow, it is an exile's dream of home. A beguiling attraction is a superb collection of miniatures — superior doll's house furniture. NT. April-October, daily except Mon and Fri but including Good Friday, 2-6; weekends and BH Mondays 12-6. £3.50, child £1.50. Garden £2.00, with children free. 01439 748283.

Ampleforth: 5m south west off B1257 Malton road. Home of the famous Roman Catholic public school and a modern Benedictine Abbey. Completed in 1961 and open to the public, the abbey's medieval-style church is by Sir Giles Gilbert Scott, who also designed Britain's traditional red phone box.

Orchard: The abbey's seven-acre apple orchard is the most northerly commercial orchard in Britain. Prearranged group visits can be made, and there are 'farmgate' sales of apples from August to April. 01439 788485

Byland Abbey: Actually at Wass, five miles from the original site near Old Byland. The monks of

Rievaulx, the earliest to arrive, objected to the new-comers' bells. The abbey's special feature is some fine tile flooring. EH, April-October, daily 10-6, November-March Wed-Sun 10-4; £1.25, concessions 95p, children 60p. 01347 869614.

KIRKBYMOORSIDE DISTRICT

Kirkbymoorside: Pop 2,645. The main-road clutter of garages and factories gives no clue to the unspoiled centre of this little town. The timbered 17th century porch of the Black Swan juts into the Market Place, and there are some charmingly old fashioned shop fronts. Buckingham House, near the King's Head hotel, is said to be where the rollicking Duke of Buckingham, founder of the Bilsdale Hunt, died in 1687 — "in the worst inn's worst room", according to a poem by Alexander Pope. Market Day Wednesday.

Ryedale Agricultural Show: Welburn Park, fourth Tuesday in July.

Appleton-le-Moors: 3m east off A 170 4m west. Distinguished by its pencil-slim spire, a landmark for miles around, the village church was built as a memorial to Joseph Shepherd, a retired shipping merchant. He collapsed and died while riding his horse in the village, his birthplace, in 1862. A trio of sculpted faces set into a cottage wall at the other end of the village depict The Three Bloodsuckers — Lawyer, Doctor and Clergyman.

Kirkdale — St. Gregory's Minster: Down a track off a sideroad from the busy A170 between Helmsley and Kirkbymoorside the secluded church of St. Gregory's has one of Britain's best preserved Saxon sundials. The priest named on its roughly-executed inscription, Brand, is the first parish priest known by name in Yorkshire. The church also retains its original Saxon wall benches. In 1821, quarrymen working nearby broke into a cave that contained the remains of animals including lion, tiger, rhino, and mammoth — inhabitants of the region before the Ice Age. An attractive three-mile woodland walk leads to

St Gregory's Minster, Kirkdale

Sleightholmedale, a sylvan lower portion of Bransdale, graced by the lovely Sleightholmedale Lodge where terraced gardens are occasionally open to the public.

Hutton-le-Hole: 4m north-east off A 170. The most "picture postcard" moorland village, with white-painted bridges spanning a beck that bisects hummocky sheep-cropped greens. On Bank Holidays it can resemble Blackpool. Most of the cottages were built by 17th century Quaker weavers. From "Quaker Cottage" in the 18th century John Richardson set out as a Quaker missionary, becoming famous in America through the white horse that carried him on his 4,000 mile odyssey.

Today's trim appearance of the village makes it hard to imagine that a century ago it was home to many hard drinking, and sometimes hard-fighting, Rosedale ironstone miners, and that as recently as 1939 gypsies camped on the greens.

Ryedale Folk Museum: Covers 2.5 acres with a variety of reconstructed buildings including, an Elizabethan manor house, thatched moorland cottage, and a unique medieval glass furnace, transferred from Rosedale. Each September it stages the World Championship of Merrills, an ancient peg-board

game. March 27-Oct, daily 10-5.30. £2.50, children
£1.25, senior citizens and students £2. 01751 417367

Lastingham: Deep in trees close to Hutton-le-
Hole, Lastingham provides a contrast in beauty to its
more open neighbour. The parish church began life as
11th century abbey, but before it was completed
attacks by marauders forced the monks to move to
York. Steps from the nave lead to the abbey's original
vaulted crypt.

In the 18th century, the wife of the parish priest ran
the Blacksmith's Arms. To supplement his meagre
stipend, her husband played his fiddle in the pub. The
church-pub link endures in the pub's own draught
beer, Church Ales, the first pint of which, drawn in
1993, was blessed by the vicar.

The lintel of a nearby house bears an inscription
with which most people would agree: The hap of a
lyfe — good or ill — the choyce of a wyfe.

Gillamoor: 2m north on local road. The bank top
near the church commands a much-photographed
"surprise view' of Farndale. The church was built sin-
gle-handedly in 1802 by a Gillamoor stonemason
James Smith. Behind the church, little-known
Douthwaite Dale, an extension of Farndale, offers a
pleasant walk to or from Kirkbymoorside.

Farndale: Reached beyond either Gillamoor or
Hutton-le-Hole. Famous for its extensive display of
wild daffodils by the river Dove. Their origin is
unknown and there is no evidence to back a theory
that they were planted by the monks of Rievaulx.

The classic 1.5 mile 'daffodil walk' links the ham-
lets of Low Mill and Church Houses. The best displays are near Church Houses, where they can be easily reached by disabled visitors, down a lane alongside
the Feversham Arms.

PICKERING DISTRICT

Pickering: Pop 6,205. A substantial but still attractive market town, whose layout, with the church at
the apex of two hills, echoes the Dales. The parish
church contains some of Britain's best preserved

medieval wall paintings. Efforts are currently being made to restore a rare modern counterpart — a mural of three children joyfully scoffing cakes. Damaged by damp, this was painted in the Memorial Hall by Rex Whistler for a children's wartime Christmas party in 1943.

Billeted in Pickering at the time, Whistler, a tank commander with the Welsh Guards, was killed shortly afterwards in the Battle of Normandy. Two 10ft-tall Whistler paintings of guardsmen, which once flanked the doors of the Memorial Hall, are exhibited in the Beck Isle Museum.

The railway station, smack in the middle of the town, is the southern terminus of the North Yorkshire Moors Railway. Engines often stand steaming right by the main crossroads.

Castle: Once the administrative centre of a vast hunting forest the castle was visited by most medieval kings. Its well-preserved outer walls and towers make the inner concourse into a suntrap — an ideal place for picnics. One tower, Rosamund's, was named in

Pickering Castle   *B. R. Hammond*

Lady Lumley's Hospital at Thornton dale

Alec Wright

honour of a popular local woman who died when she
was forced by Henry II's wife to drink a cup of poi-
son — her punishment for being Henry's mistress.
EH April-Oct daily 10-6, Nov-March, Wed-Sun, 10-
4. £1.80, child 90p, concessions £1.35. 01751
474989

Beck Isle Museum: Located in the home of 18th
century agricultural pioneer William Marshall, the
museum fittingly emphasises local rural history. Of
exceptional interest are the nostalgic countryside photographs of Sydney Smith, a Pickering commercial
photographer (1884-1956). Easter/April-October,
daily 10-5. £1.75, children 65p, concessions £1.50.
0751 473653

Annual attractions: Trucking festival — second
weekend in June. Traction engine rally, Fri-Sun last
weekend in July. Admission to both, adult £4, child
£1, family £8.

Cinema: Castle, Castlegate. 01751 472622.

Market day Monday. EC Wed.

TIC: Eastgate Car Park. March-October, daily
9.30-6; November-February, Mon-Sat 10-4.30.
01751 473791

Cropton: 5m west off A 170. A pleasant hilltop village overlooking Rosedale. There's a castle mound, and in the churchyard the stump of a cross where a flagon of water was kept to slake the thirst of travellers. Today's visitors can enjoy beer brewed at the pub, the New Inn.

In woods towards Sinnington, a low white cottage, Nutholme, was the birthplace of Whitby's two great whaling skippers, William Scoresby Senior and Junior.

Rosedale: 2m north of Cropton on local road — or by steep 'Chimney Bank' road, between Hutton-le-Hole and Lastingham. "Rossi's Valley" — an old Norse personal name, nothing to do with roses. And today's Rosedale Abbey is a village, partly grouped round a sleepy square.

The school playground doubles as the forecourt of the church, across which coffins had to be carried until new arrangements were made recently. A path by the church door passes the stump of a tower which is all that survives of the 'abbey', in reality a 12th century nunnery.

The ruin was heavily plundered during Rosedale's epic 19th century ironstone boom, when the population multiplied to around 5,000. Three sets of enormous crumbling kilns, one of which is belatedly being conserved, are dotted around the valley.

The 12-mile long trackbed of the railway by which the ore was despatched across the moors to the blast-furnaces of the North-East, is now a superb walkers' route.

Wildflower and Herb Nursery: Pot-grown wild flowers of the moors for sale. High Farm, Hartoft. 01751 417648.

Agricultural Show: Usually third Sat in August.

Cawthorne Camps: About 2 miles east of the village. Covering more than 100 acres, the apparent muddle of earthworks is four Roman army training camps — among the best of their kind in the Roman Empire. A one-mile waymarked walk goes round two of the camps, which are permanently open. No charge.

Thornton-le-Dale: 2m east. Voted Yorkshire's prettiest village in 1911 and has never really recovered: Thornton is the Windermere of the Moors.

Most of its many visitors do little except snap the dormered thatched cottage, perfectly situated on a bend of a beck, wander past more rose-clad beckside cottages, and patronise the numerous gift shops and tearooms.

The short path to Ellerburn introduces a different world — a tranquil haven with a Saxon church, in the pulpit of which a caretaker's hens once hatched chickens. Buried at Thornton church is Matthew Grimes, a guard of Napoleon on St. Helena.

Show: Midweek early August. Phone Pickering TIC.

Dalby Forest: Off local road 1m north of Thornton Dale or from Fox and Rabbit Inn on A169 5m north of Pickering. Nature trails, a cycle route and a forest drive are among the many features of this popular recreation area.

Visitor Centre and Museum: In Dalby Village, 3m north of Thornton-le-Dale. Easter-October, 11-5. 0751 460295. Or Forest Enterprise Pickering office, 0751 472771.

Bridestones: Naturally-weathered sandstone outcrops of intriguing shape — i.e. The Mustard Pot. The name is derived from a Norse word meaning "brink". Part of a National Trust nature reserve the stones can be reached by road from the Dalby Forest drive.

Lockton and Levisham: 5m north off A169 5m north. Always considered together though separated by the deep valley of Levisham Beck. A rowan by Lockton church gate was planted there after being removed from the top of the church tower, where it appears in old prints. At Stothard's garage a 1926 hand-operated petrol pump is still in service, delivering diesel.

An eccentric 19th century Levisham squire and rector, Robert Skelton, built a tower now named after him as a lodge in which he could sleep on the moors during the grouse shooting season. Set on the edge of

A bridestone above Dovedale and Staindale

Ken Paver

Newton Dale it is a good vantage point for the North Yorkshire Moors Railway.

Hole of Horcum: 7m north by A169. Moorland springs are the unlikely agents that carved this great amphitheatre. But it is nice to believe that a giant scooped up a handful of earth to create his punch-bowl. The nearby pudding shaped hill Blakey Topping is obviously the discarded earth. There are walks through the Hole and round its rim — the best aiming for Levisham.

TOWARDS SCARBOROUGH

Ebberston Hall: By the A170 between Pickering and Scarborough. What looks like a baroque gate-house is England's smallest stately home. But Ebberston village was moved to create an unblemished view from this mini Castle Howard, built in 1718 for the girlfriend of a local MP. Ungratefully, she never even came to see it.

A strange habit of a 19th century owner, squire George Osbaldeston, was tracing the outline of his girlfriends' hands and feet on the lead roof, where some still exist.

Behind the house are attractive water gardens. Open Bank Holidays or by appointment, 10-5. £2.50. 01723 859057.

Brompton: On A170 between Pickering and Scarborough. Brompton Hall, now a special school, is where George Cayley, the aviation pioneer, built a virtual forerunner of the modern airplane, 50 years before the Wright Brothers achieved powered flight. In 1853 Cayley's machine carried his coachman across Brompton Dale, prompting the servant to resign with the words: "I was hired to drive not fly."

Gallows Hill: The poet William Wordsworth came to this farmhouse in October 1802 to marry the farmer's daughter Mary Hutchinson.

An exhibition celebrates this link, and a similar salute to George Cayley is planned. Daily 10-5. 01723 863298.

Hackness: The centrepiece of the richly wooded Forge Valley, with pretty cottages and a handsome Hall, the home of Lord Derwent. The beautiful

Castle Howard   *Bertram Unne*

church contains stones from a nunnery that existed here from 680-869.

MALTON DISTRICT

Malton: On the edge of the Wolds but also handy for the Moors, Malton is relatively free from tourists — and none the worse for that. Its town centre cattle market (Mon, Tues, Fri) fills the town with farmers. The Midland Bank bears a grape vine whose harvest is shared among staff.

Charles Dickens wrote part of Martin Chuzzlewit while staying with a Malton solicitor. The setting of his former office, a passageway called Chancery Lane, is said to have been the model for Scrooge's dingy workplace.

In Norton, immediately across the river, there are several racing stables, and the exercising of horses is an everyday sight.

Town Museum, Market Place: Chiefly reflects Malton's importance as a Roman town. Easter-Oct, Mon-Sat 10-4, Sun 2-4. 90p, children/Senior citizens 60p, family £2.50. 01653 695136.

Cinema: The Palace, Yorkersgate. 01653 600008

Ryedale Festival: Large programme of professional arts events staged throughout Ryedale during the last week in July and first in August. Festival office, Ryedale House, Malton. 01653 600666 ext 268.

TIC: Market Place. March-October, daily 9.30-5.30; November-February part time. 01653 600048.

Castle Howard, near Malton: Major stately home, amazingly the first building designed by soldier-play-wright Sir John Vanbrugh. Now internationally famous as the setting of TV's Brideshead Revisited it still the family home of the Howards. March 18-October, daily, grounds and gardens from 10, house from 11. 01653 648333.

Eden Camp: Off A169 Malton-Pickering road. World War II theme park, developed at former PoW camp. Mid February-December 23, 10-5. 01653 697777.

Eden Farm: Working farm with display areas and exhibitions. Early Spring to last Sun in October.

01653 692093.

Flamingoland, Kirbymisperton, near Malton: Fun park with over 100 rides, and Europe's largest privately-owned zoo. Easter-October 2, from 10 am, plus weekends and October half term. 01653 668287.

3 THE COAST

by Harry Mead

The inspiration of Captain Cook, the ideal home of Britain's largest seabird, the playground of millions. Fought over, ravaged by industry, yet bright with wild flowers. If Britain has a greater coast of contrasts than Yorkshire's it must be awaiting a new Captain Cook to discover it.

Just north of the fishing village of Staithes, which marks the county's boundary with Cleveland, Boulby Cliff soars to 679ft. England's second highest cliff, and the highest on the East Coast, it peers down on

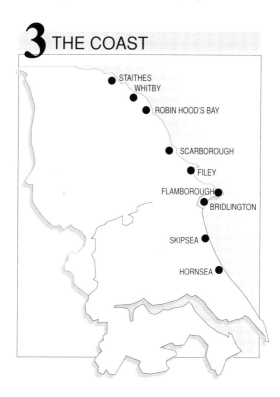

3 THE COAST

STAITHES
WHITBY
ROBIN HOOD'S BAY
SCARBOROUGH
FILEY
FLAMBOROUGH
BRIDLINGTON
SKIPSEA
HORNSEA

the seemingly squared-off headland of Cowbar Nab,
the main bulwark defending Staithes. Southwards,
steep cliffs run almost uninterruptedly for the best
part of 40 miles. Before petering out beyond
Bridlington, they produce another superlative. The
420-ft white cliffs of Bempton, twice as high as York
Minster, stand taller than any other chalk cliffs in
Britain. Catching the eye of motorists on the
Pickering-Scarborough road some 20 miles away their
gleaming wall is pockmarked with the ledges and
crannies chosen by the gannet, our largest seabird, for
its only mainland nesting site. From February to
August some 800 pairs mingle with around 200,000
other breeding birds in England's biggest bird colony.

Until 1955, when the Wild Birds' Protection Act
came into force, local cliff-climbers, known as
climmers, perilously descended on ropes to collect the

Whitby Harbour   *C. Haines*

birds' eggs, sold as delicacies. Today the only death-defying feat is the gannet's headlong plunge into the waves. One of Britain's most breathtaking wildlife sights this is easily seen from the clifftop.

But it was at Staithes that young James Cook felt the pull of the sea. Born and raised in Cleveland farming country, at 16 he went to work as a grocer's assistant in Staithes. He slept, it is said, under the shop's counter. The roar of the sea pounding the makeshift wall just yards away would have terrified many. But Cook knew his destiny lay out there.

Within 18 months he was apprenticed to a Whitby shipowner. He lodged in his master's house, overlooking the shipyards where the colliers that were to carry him around the world were built. The house is now open to the public. In its large attic (the apprentices' dormitory) it is easy to picture young Cook and the other novice seamen bedding down on their straw pallets.

Crammed on to the steep banks of the only natural refuge along the 100 miles of coast between the Tees and Humber, Whitby is instantly identifiable. Nowhere else do a parish church and abbey share an exposed clifftop, reached on foot by a prominent curving stone stairway: visitors must count every one of the 199 steps, and those who get it wrong must start again. Down at the harbour an antique bridge, straight from the Willow Pattern, holds together, and yet divides, the two distinct parts of the town.

When closed, this 1908 swinging contraption links the ancient East Side and more recent West like the clasp of a cherished old brooch. When the bell on its turreted bridge house announces its imminent opening, to allow vessels to pass to or from the upper harbour, the bridge is suddenly filled with folk who, observed from elsewhere around the harbour, look like scurrying Lowry-like matchstick figures, eager to cross before the town is split asunder.

The winter atmosphere in Whitby, when few tourists wander its web of cobbled streets and yards and twisting stairways, and the summer yachtsmen have left the harbour to the local fishing fleet, is probably not greatly different from how Cook knew it. Certainly it comes close to the spirit of a late Victorian seaport captured in the photographs of Frank Sutcliffe. Perhaps Whitby's most popular souvenirs these are sold in a purpose-built gallery.

Once big in whaling, and famous for the manufacture of jewellery from jet, the black gemstone mined locally and popularised by the mourning Queen Victoria, Whitby didn't get into tourism until the railway arrived in 1847. But the coast's premier resort, Scarborough has a different story to tell.

When a mineral spring was discovered in 1620, it looked set to become a spa. Thirty years later local GP Dr Wittie began vigorously advocating the then new practice of sea bathing. So Scarborough, with a history dating back to a Bronze Age settlement on its Castle headland, emerged as Britain's first seaside resort.

Shown on prints of the South Bay in 1828, the mobile bathing hut might have been born there. England's first cliff lift, one of three still operating in the resort, was installed at the Spa in 1875.

Often collectively described as 'Cornish', the coast's three outstanding villages also have distinct personalities. Staithes, with gulls screaming everywhere, is rugged and dour. It has never lost the feel of a working place.

Runswick Bay, more open and sunny, gazes across a bay which can, and sometimes does, look Mediterranean. Robin Hood's Bay, though in a cleft like Staithes, is the outstandingly pretty one. Its steep street plunges straight to the beach, and in its little squares you will find climbing roses and tubs of flowers — trimmings still foreign to tough old Staithes. But Bay, as the village is called, was once a bigger fishing centre even than Whitby.

Only there and at Scarborough is fishing now a significant 'industry.' But virtually every coastal community still maintains a small fleet of Yorkshire cobles, fishing the inshore waters. Derived from the Viking

Robin Hood's Bay   *Den Oldroyd*

longboat the design of this high-prowed, partly flat
bottomed craft evolved to cope with operating directly off tidal beaches. In bays constantly gnawed at by
the sea these are enclosed by bold headlands.

But until most of the coast was recently awarded
'heritage' status, beauty never counted for much. The
bare headland at Sandsend is the degraded outcome
of the extraction of alum, a mineral used in tanning,
dyeing and the production of medicines. Carried out
widely in the North York Moors between the 16th
and 19th centuries, alum-refining was a particularly
noxious process. The remains of works recently
restored by the National Trust are now on view near
Ravenscar, and walkers on Boulby Cliff can also visit
a set of mighty stone vats, rightly likened by one
observer to "relics of the Aztecs".

But Nature brings delight. On the Flamborough

cliffs near Speeton, orchids bloom with such vigour that two species, the Fragrant and Pyramid, have formed a dramatic, tall hybrid. And yet not far away, above Thornwick Bay, the strength of winter gales is measured in the presence, almost on the 390ft clifftop, of Sea Arrow, a grass that depends on salt spray. Further north, approaching Ravenscar, orchids again flourish, this time including the secretive Frog Orchid, so named because of the shape and colour of its tiny green flowers.

The invading Romans would breach the so called Danes Dyke, an Iron Age earthwork defending Flamborough Head. In turn they were overwhelmed. At Goldsborough, north of Whitby, the end apparently came with brutal suddenness. From a grass-covered fort archaeologists unearthed the skeleton of a man, with a knife buried in his back by another man, whose neck was gripped by the skeleton of a large dog.

Centuries later more coastal drama came out of the blue. With the First World War only 14 weeks old, two German warships emerged from the early morning December mist and pounded Whitby and Scarborough. Unused barracks at Scarborough Castle were destroyed, bits were knocked off the west end of Whitby Abbey, and 21 people died. Never properly explained, the attack gave mainland Britain its first taste of world war.

The coast from north to south

Staithes: The uninviting assortment of semis, estates, and former ironstone mining terraces at Staithes' Bank Top, give no hint that down an unseen 1-4 hill lies one of the most atmospheric of fishing villages. Wedged into a cleft between two bluff headlands Staithes is strong and stern. To find the best-known bird's eye view cross a footbridge down an obscure passage where the road bends near the Post Office, and climb to Cowbar Cottages. This also reveals the safe moorings of the fishing cobles, on

Roxby Beck. The famous fishwives' bonnet, worn to protect the hair when carrying baited lines or baskets, is now rarely seen, but souvenir examples are on sale at Lawson's gift shop, where they are made by Ann Lawson.

The harbourside shop where the future Captain Cook worked as a grocer's assistant was long ago claimed by the sea, which has twice wrecked the jutting out Cod and Lobster pub. Nearby, just above the misleadingly named Captain Cook's Cottage, an 18" wide passage, Dog Loup, is the adventurous possible start of an alternative return route to the car park, climbing a narrow stepped lane to another fine viewpoint. The belching chimney on the landward side belongs to Britain's only potash mine, whose 1,400ft shaft is the deepest in Europe.

Captain Cook and Staithes Heritage Centre: Methodist Chapel. Memorabilia and Victorian re-creations, including fishermen's warehouse and chandlery, Daily 10-5.

Events: Shanty weekend. End April-May. Street performance of shanties by groups including the Staithes Fishermen's Choir. Lifeboat Day. Late July or early August. The bonnets come out for this one, which also features imaginative shop window displays.

Port Mulgrave: In the 1850s ironmaster Sir Charles Palmer built breakwaters to form a harbour for the shipment of iron ore to Tyneside. The trade was abandoned in 1916 and the breakwaters are now little more than rubble. Nearby, the blocked up exit of a tunnel through which the ore, mined three miles inland, was transported to the harbour, can still be seen.

Runswick Bay: More open than Staithes, Runswick climbs the cliffs instead of being crannied into them. A thatched cottage with the sea almost lapping its walls symbolises its fair face. And yet it struggles to survive. In 1682 the entire village collapsed into the sea. The present road and sea wall were built following a major landslip of 1968. Though ignored by the Cleveland Way the abandoned old road is the best path into the village, where most houses are holiday homes. But the community maintains a proud lifeboat tradition. Runswick women once launched the boat, and when the RNLI withdrew its lifeboat in 1978 villagers provided their own, an inshore craft whose replacement is on duty today.

Kettleness: A victim of coast erosion, which is gobbling the cliffs at a rate of three inches a year. In a sudden loss of 1829 the entire Kettleness hamlet slid down the cliff. The residents had just enough warning to escape.

Sandsend: Literally the end of a three mile stretch of sand from Whitby. With 'facilities' kept at the bucket-and-spade level, the beach is popular with families. Clustered round two becks, the village is sheltered to the north by the woods of Mulgrave Castle. Lord Normanby opens these to the public, free of charge, on Wednesdays and weekends except in May. They are place of local pilgrimage in February when the banksides of a ruined Norman castle are clothed with snowdrops.

In mid Victorian times the Maharaja Duleep Singh rented the modern castle. He built the coast road to Whitby, but the legend that this was because he kept elephants which didn't like sand between their toes is sadly untrue.

Whitby: Pop 13,500. A matchless townscape and exceptionally rich history make Whitby one of the most fascinating of all Britain's small towns.

Abbey: St Hilda founded the first in 657. The method of fixing Easter was settled there in 664 — and has remained a mystery ever since. Destroyed by the Danes in 867 it was succeeded in the 11th century by the present abbey, whose dramatic ruins dominate the clifftop. Its tyrannical rule of the neighbourhood made it hated, and locals felt a great yoke had been lifted when it was dissolved in 1539. EH. April -Sept, daily, 10-6, October-March daily 10-1, 2-4. £1.50, children 75p, concessions £1.10. 01947 603568.

St. Mary's Church, Whitby   *Brian Breton*

St. Mary's Parish Church: Often assumed to belong to the abbey, Whitby's famous 199 steps are properly the 'church stairs' — the amazing approach to one of England's most remarkable churches. Ship's carpenters fashioned its interior, fitting rows of 'cabin lights', or windows, round the roof. The bond with the sea is also expressed in penknife carvings of ships on some pews — probably the work of bored apprentices.

Captain Cook Memorial Museum: Grape Lane. Apprentice seaman James Cook lodged here, the elegant harbourside home of his shipowner employer John Walker. Furnished in period style it contains displays on Cook's life and voyages. April-October, daily 9.45-4.30; March and November weekends 11-3, £1.50, Senior citizens and children £1, family £4. 01947 601900

Museum and Art Gallery: Pannet Park. Happily unmodernised 'treasure-house' type Museum. Immense fossilised reptiles on the wall overlook oddities like Dr Merryweather's Tempest Prognosticator, a weather forecasting contraption that was activated by locally-caught leeches. Special displays on whaling and Cook. The art gallery has many lovely paintings of the district. May-Sept, Mon-Sat 9.30-5.30, Sun 2-5; Oct-April, Mon, Tues 10.30-1, Wed-Sat 10.30-4, Sun 2-4. Museum £1, child 50p; art gallery free. 01947 602908

Lifeboat Museum: Pier Road. Whitby's lifeboat station has earned more gold and silver medals than any other in Britain. Besides relics from many heroic

Caedmon, at the top of Abbey Steps, Whitby

rescues the museum contains Britain's last oar-powered lifeboat, on duty at Whitby until 1957. Easter-October daily 10-6. Nov-Easter, daily subject to weather 11-4. No charge. 01947 602001.

Victorian Jet Works: Church St. In the late 19th century the manufacture of jewellery from jet, a gemstone formed from fossilised wood, was Whitby's main industry. The various stages of manufacture are all represented. An incorporated shop is one of several that sells contemporary jet jewellery, still made on a small scale in Whitby. Daily from 9.30. 50p, children and senior citizens 30p. 01947 8215300.

Pictorial Archives, Grape Lane. Wide-ranging collection of local historic photos. daily 10.30-4.30. Free 01947 600170.

Dracula Experience: Marine Parade. Re-creates

episodes from Bram Stoker's novel, part of which is set in Whitby. March-Sept, daily except Friday. Adults £1.75, Senior citizens and children £1.25. 0947 601923. There is also a Dracula Trail leaflet at TIC.

Museum of Victorian Whitby, Sandgate: Another theme attraction using modern techniques. Children can take the helm of a whaling ship in a howling gale. March-December, and winter weekends, from 9.30. £1.75, Senior citizens £1, children 90p, family £5.50. 01947 601221.

Entertainments: Pavilion complex, West Cliff. shows, dances, concerts etc. 01947 604855. Cinema — The Coliseum, Victoria Square.

Market Day: Saturday.

Miscellaneous: Fortune's Kippers, Henrietta St. Kippers smoked in tarred shed, their fragrance filling the street and drifting up to clifftop St. Mary's. Botham's Bakery Baxtergate and Flowergate: their lemon buns and butter buns are as much local delicacies as crab. Magpie Cafe, Pier Road, award winning fish restaurant, run by same family since 1948. Old Smugglers, Baxtergate. Perfect inglenook tearoom in former 15th century Ship Launch Inn.

Whalebone Arch, West Cliff — commemorates Whitby's whaling days and frames perfectly-composed view of abbey and church. Nearby, a fine bronze statute of Cook gazes steadfastly to sea.

Missions to Seamen building, Haggersgate — a Whitby surprise, this imposing house of former shipowner John Yeoman could deputise for York's Mansion House.

Events: Annual Eskdale Arts Festival — May; Whitby Festival — June; Regatta — early August; Folk Week — late August. Lifeboat Day — late August. Details from TIC, 01947 602674, except Folk event 01482 634742, and Lifeboat 01947 602216.

TIC: Langborne Rd. Daily, May-Sept 9.30-6, October-April 10-12, 1-4.30. 01947 602674

Robin Hood's Bay: The name's origin is mystery, and it is unlikely that the outlaw either kept a boat here as an ultimate means of escape, or came here to help the Whitby Abbot repel invaders. Locals simply call it Bay. Now considered an epitome of "picturesque" its stacked-up cottages struck the writer of a 17th century guidebook as "grotesque." In the 19th century it had more fishing boats than Whitby — 50 in 1814 — and smuggling was big too. Some cottages have interconnecting doors masquerading as cupboards, and it is said that a smuggled cask of brandy or bale of silk could pass from the sea to the clifftop without seeing daylight.

In the last 200 years 200 houses have fallen into the sea, and King St., which now ends at a 40ft seawall built in 1975 was once the main road to Whitby. The beach and cliffs are a favourite fossil hunting ground.

Museum: The Reading Room, Fisherhead. Its display on ganseys, fishermen's jerseys, reveals that their patterns helped to identify drowned men. There is also an account of an 1821 lifeboat rescue, in which the lifeboat was hauled six miles overland from Whitby. Daily except Saturday, June-September 1.30-4, July-August 11-4. 25p, child 5p.

Smuggling Experience: Warehouse, Banktop. Modern theme museum on three floors. Easter-October daily 10-6. £2, Senior citizens and children £1. 01947 880168.

Ravenscar: Known as rokes, the sea frets that hang about this 600ft headland are said to have given Bram Stoker the idea for setting part of his novel Dracula in nearby Whitby. In real life, the 1774 mock-battlemented Raven Hall was a convenient place to conceal the feeble-minded George III (1738-1820), whose personal physician owned the hall. In 1895 a new resort was planned here, but only one or two villas, and some roads, now leading nowhere, were built. Those sea frets put off investors.

National Trust Coastal Centre: Excellent displays on history, wildlife and geology. Booklet on 3-mile geological trail. April-Sept 10.30-5.30. 01723 870138

Peak Alum Works: Active for almost two centuries

(1673-1864) these works were among about ten in the moors which converted alum shale into crystals, used mainly to fix colours in tanning and dyeing. The extensive remains give a comprehensive picture of the process, so vile that the local rain turned acid. But the finished product was so precious that some works were protected by guards. NT. Open all year, information on site. Free.

Hayburn Wyke: The Tropics come to the Yorkshire Coast. Victorians ran rail excursions to this lush inlet, watered by a stream that cascades on to the stoney beach, and with old woodland sheltering a wealth of moisture loving plants. The lovely Grass of Parnassus, like a mini Christmas Rose, is one of its beauties, but best is the fraternity of foxgloves, flowering in a hillside birch wood.

Scarborough: Pop 53,500. A Viking raider, Scarthi, gave his name to what became, and many would say still is, The Queen of Watering Places. Linked by a scenic Marine Drive round its rocky castle-crowned Headland, its two bays can satisfy most tastes. There are extensive gardens, some terraced into the cliffs, a 'golden half-mile' of slot machines, shellfish stalls, two extensive sandy beaches.

The many attractions for children include a minature railway that runs nearly a mile to Scalby Mills, an out-lier of Scarborough with a fun park, and unique naval warfare — a battle fought by large model warships in Peasholm Park. Some visitors go just for the

North Yorkshire Coast   *Den Oldroyd*

county cricket, others for the plays of Alan Ayckbourn, who lives in the town and premiers most of his plays there. "If you can make the Scarborough audience laugh you can make them laugh anywhere," he says. Hmm....

Art Gallery: The Crescent. Fine collection includes atmospheric oil paintings of Victorian Scarborough by the "wizard of moonlight", Leeds-born Atkinson Grimshaw. All year — Tues-Sat, plus Bank Holidays, 10-1, 2-5, Sundays 2.5. Free. 01723 374753

Castle: Founded 12th century. Shares headland with scanty remains of 4th century Roman Signal Tower. Picnickers welcome. EH. April-Oct 10-6; Nov-March 10-4. £1.50, concession £1.10, children 75p. 01723 372451.

Peasholm Park: "If it were secluded and aristocratic it would be much admired." So says Barbara Jones in her book Follies and Grottoes. Instead, Peasholm Park, with its Japanese theme buildings and lanterns on poles slanting over the boating lake, is public and popular — one of Yorkshire's best-loved places. Setting of band concerts and the famous naval warfare, and the seaward end of a peaceful woodland walk through Peasholm Glen, the park was fashioned from an area of piggeries in 1912.

Rotunda Museum: Vernon Road. One of Britain's first purpose-built museums — opened 1829. Mainly archaeology. All year Tues-Sat, plus BHs, 10-5; Sundays 2-5. Free. 01723 374839

Woodend Museum: The Crescent. Natural history, former home of the literary Sitwell family. For opening times phone 01723 367326.

Millenium: The Foreshore. Scarborough's history presented in the modern mix of sound, vision, and life-size models. Daily except Christmas Day, 10am to 10pm in main holiday season, 10 — 6 other times. £3.50, children £2, concession £3. 01723 501000

Maritime Experience: Lighthouse Pier. Maritime history on a converted deep sea trawler. For times and charges phone 01723 353333

Kinderland: Burniston Road. Four-acre fun park,

Flamborough Head   *F. L. Jackson*

partly in landscaped woodland, with emphasis on activity — canoeing, trampolining, castle-building etc.

Sea trips: In pleasure craft Coronia and Regal Lady. 01723 871186.

Sealife Centre: Scalby Mills. 70 species of sea creature, in displays that replicate their natural habitats. Daily except Christmas Day 10-6, £4.35, Senior citizens £3.25, children £2.25.

Entertainments: Cinemas — Hollywood Plaza, North Marine Road, 01723 365119; Opera House, Thomas St. 0723 369999; Theatres-Futurist, Foreshore Road, 01723 365789. Stephen Joseph Theatre-in-the Round (home of Alan Ayckbourn plays), Valley Bridge Parade. Backstage tours are available. 01723 370541. YMCA Theatre, Thomas St., mainly amateur, 01723 374227. Superbowl — Foreshore Road, 01723 377960. Spa complex —

largest venue in town, 01723 376774.

Events: Motor racing — several car and motorcycle events on Oliver's Mount. For details phone Scarborough TIC 0723 373333, or 0377 154727. Naval warfare Peasholm Park, selected dates to end of June then Mon and Thurs afternoons till early Sept, £1.20, children 60p. Band concerts — Sunday afternoons, Peasholm Park from late May to early September, 80p, children 10p. Cricket: Several Yorkshire fixtures and two-week festival starting in late August. 0723 365625. Scarborough Fayre: mid to end of June, street performances, parades etc.

Parish Church: St Mary's, by the castle. The churchyard contains the grave of Ann Bronte. Sheltered walls in the churchyard are the remains of the original chancel, destroyed during a 17-month seige of the castle in 1644-5.

Market Day: Thurs; EC Wed.

TIC: St. Nicholas Cliff. Daily, May-Sept 9.30-6, Oct-April 10-4.30. 01723 373333

Nearby: Shire Horse Farm, Staintondale, off A171 Whitby Road. Visitors can pat the gentle giants, feed the farm ducks and hens, follow a clifftop trail and (at certain times), enjoy a horse-and-cart ride. Easter and May-early Oct, Sun, Tues, Wed, Fri, and BHs 10.30-4.30. £2.50, Senior citizens £2, children £1.50. 01723 870548. Honey Farm: Betton Farm, East Ayton, on A170 Pickering road. Claimed to be "probably the world's best exhibition of the living Honey Bee." Daily 10-5, £1.50, Senior citizens and children £1, family £5. 01723 863143.

Filey: Pop. 6,600. With a six mile crescent of hard firm sand fringing a spacious bay, Filey has kept itself simple. A favourite of the Bronte sisters, it remains a classic place for people who like a quiet seaside holiday — with or without bucket and spade. The sands terminate near the town in the striking rock promontory of The Brigg, a threequarter-mile long reef, mostly submerged at high tide. In legend it was an attempt by the Devil to bridge the North Sea.

Evidence of a pier that once jutted from the Brigg

suggests it could have been the Roman landing point identified in their history as "a well havened bay." So a plan once put forward to develop a harbour capable of berthing the entire British Fleet perhaps isn't surprising. An appealing feature in the town are stained glass panels of fishing boats fitted in many doors. Cliff House, where the Brontes stayed, is now a cafe, where diners relax beneath an ancient far-spreading grape vine.

Museum: Queen St. In Filey's oldest (1696) cottage. Displays on fishing, lifeboats, etc. May-Sept except Sat, 2-5. 40p, children 20p. 01723 513640.

Entertainments: Cinema The Grand, Union St. 01723 512129; Theatre Sun Lounge, Crescent Gardens. Intimate theatre and cabaret venue. O1723 512129

Events: Edwardian Festival — late June early July. 01723 516142. Band concerts — Summer Sundays in Crescent Gardens. Lifeboat Day — late July or early August, 01723 513401. Fishing Festival: First week in September. Attracts 1,500 anglers, fishing from the Brigg. 01723 515532.

TIC: John St. 01723 512204. Has pamphlet on 2 mile nature trail along and around the Brigg. Also details of key hire for Brigg bird hide.

Nearby. Hunmanby (3 miles) is an attractive Wolds

Runswick Bay   *Bernard Fearnley*

Staithes

village. The nearby Hunmanby Gap, with a popular Beach Cafe, is another access to Filey Bay sands. Bempton — see below.

Bempton Cliffs: Between 2,000 and 4,000 puffins; 3,000 razorbills; 10,000 — 15,000 guillemots, 85,000 kittiwakes. . . the numbers spell out the scale of this seabird city, England's biggest seabird colony, on the last seabird cliffs down Britain's East Coast. Centred on Bempton, whose towering chalk buttresses are twice as high as York Minster, they stretch for some six miles from Speeton to Flamborough Head.

One hundred and sixty species have been recorded, of which about 33 breed regularly. The most spectacular, the gannet, our biggest seabird, nests nowhere else on mainland Britain. Most of the 800 or so pairs are on Bempton Cliffs, which attract some 70,000 of the full summer contingent of around 200,000 birds. The most active period is April-July. Viewing points can be reached via a lane from Bempton — but take a nosepeg. (For sea trips to Bempton see Bridlington — Pleasure Steamers).

Flamborough Head: On its 170ft plateau, defended on three sides by cliffs and on the other by the pre-historic Danes Dyke, Flamborough village is an interesting network of squares and open spaces. A farming atmosphere pervades the part near St. Oswald's Church, whose monuments include an effigy of Sir Marmaduke Constable, complete with the toad on which he choked to death. A set of water colour panels by a local artist records Flamborough during the Second World War, with lifeboatmen plucking three airmen from the waves, and people serving tea to victims of bombing raids.

Only recently withdrawn, Flamborough's seagoing lifeboat was based at North Landing, a picturesque cove, where cobles operate from the beach. Some offer pleasure trips, an opportunity to see the superb cliff scenery — stacks, coves, arches, sheer walls. At low tide one glistening cavern, Robin Lyth's Cave, can be explored from the beach, and others can be found towards the shingly Thornwick Bay. On a chalk bed, the sea at Flamborough is Yorkshire's clearest and bluest. Grey seals and porpoises sport offshore, and the rock-pool life includes the pretty dahlia and sea anenome. Car parks at the North Landing, the more open South Landing, where the inshore lifeboat is stationed, and by the ancient chalk lighthouse and its Victorian successor, are access points for paths round the headland, suitable for wheelchairs. The partly-wooded 2-mile Danes Dyke, home to roe deer and an abundance of wildflowers, can also be explored.

Heritage Coast Information Centre: South Landing. Displays and leaflets on geology, history, and wildlife of the 12-mile Flamborough Heritage Coast. Easter-Sept weekends, plus midweek afternoons in school holidays. 01262 850819.

Bridlington: Pop 32,000. 'Brid' is two places in one. Focussed on a harbour dating back to at least the 12th century, the modern resort of Bridlington suddenly gives way, half a mile inland, to the original town. This retains some elegant 18th century houses and Edwardian shop fronts, notably 'Mr Elliott's', the chemists. But Brid's pride and joy are the safe sandy beaches that run for a mile on each side of the harbour, overlooked by its newly-refurbished promenades. A viewing platform enables visitors to watch fish being landed.

Priory: Church Green. Because it was shared by the local community, the Priory Church escaped complete destruction when the priory was dissolved in 1539. Its nave is now the parish church. Guided tours: May-Sept, Mon-Fri 10-4, Sat 10-12 and 2.30-4; October-April Mon-Sat 10-12. Free. 01262 676158 or 678410

Bayle Gate Museum: Kirkgate. The 14th century priory gatehouse houses a museum of local antiquities, plus military exhibits by the Green Howards, which has strong connections with East Yorkshire. June-Sept Tue-Thurs 2-4.30, and 7pm-9pm. £1, children 20p. 01262 603170.

Harbour Museum and Aquarium: Harbour Road. Outlines the history of the harbour.Models show the various fishing methods along the Yorkshire coast. Easter-May daily 10-dusk, June-Sept 10am-9pm; October 10-dusk. Nov-Dec Sundays only 11-dusk. 40p, children 20p 01262 670148.

Pleasure Steamers: North Pier. One-hour cruises to Flamborough Head. April-October, 10.30am-9pm, cruise times governed by tides. 01262 603081 (Yorkshire Belle) or 01262 601013 (Flamborian). Between May and October special bird-watching trips, one of three hours, another up to four, are run by the RSPB. Details from RSPB North Office, E Floor, Milburn House, Dean Street, Newcastle-upon-Tyne, NE1 1LE, 0191 232 4148.

Entertainments: The Spa. Off South Marine Road. Includes dual purpose cinema and theatre and 1,800-seat Royal Halls. There is also a restaurant and children's play area. 01262 678258.

Leisure World: The Esplanade. Four leisure pools, plus roller rink, aerobics etc. Daily from ten. Price details — 01262 606715.

Harem Leisure Park Royal Princes Parade. Despite the raunchy promise of the name, here is another

Family Fun Park. March-October 10am-late. Free entry, with token system inside. O1262 606042

Annual Events: Bridlington Festival — late April early May. Lifeboat Day — mid August. Yachting Regatta — third week in August. Sea Angling Week — mid September. Details from TIC-01262 673474.

Market Day: Wed and Sat and BH Mon.

TIC: 25, Prince St. Easter-Sept daily 9.30-5.30 (5 on Sun), Sept-Easter same except closed Sun. 01262 673474/606383.

Nearby: World of Rock. Lancaster Road, Carnaby, off A166 Driffield Road. See rock, fudge and toffee being made. Better still, roll your own piece of rock with your initial running through it. Easter-October daily 10-5; November-Easter, Mon-Fri 10.30-4. Free. 01262 678525

Sewerby Hall and Gardens: Off B1255 2 miles NW of Bridlington. Council-owned Georgian mansion and 50 acres of parkland. Museum includes room devoted to Hull-born Amy Johnson (1904-41) the first woman to fly solo from England to Australia. Open all year. £2, Senior citizens £1.50, children £1. 01262 673769. Bondville Miniature Village. At Sewerby, 1m along coast road. Stone-faced buildings and Lilliputian figures on a one-acre site. Daily May-October 10am-8pm, £2.50, children and concessions

Flamborough

£1. 01262 401736.

Sledmere House: Off B1253 15 miles west. 18th century mansion, home of Sir Tatton Sykes. Pipe organ played twice daily. £3, Senior citizens £2.50, children £1.75. Park and gardens £1.50 and £1. 01377 236637. In Sledmere village, impressive Wagoners' War Memorial. Carved with First World War scenes it honours the dead of a special regiment of 1,200 wagoners recruited from the North and East Ridings, by Sledmere's Sir Mark Sykes to provide transport in the war. Burton Agnes Hall. Off A166 5m from Bridlington. Elizabethan Hall, with gardens including a maze and giant board game. £3, Senior citizens £2.50; children £2. 01262 490324.

Rudston Monolith: Off B1253, 5 miles west of Bridlington. Britain's tallest standing stone, a prehistoric pillar 25ft high and 6ft wide, the monolith dominates the churchyard. Its purpose is unknown but the stone is believed to have been cut from a gritstone outcrop at Cayton Bay, 10 miles away near Scarborough. Buried in the churchyard is Winifred Holtby (1898-1935) author of the novel South Riding. Another grave has a well-sculpted figure of a short-trousered schoolboy — the touching memorial to ten-year-old Alastair John Thompson, who died in 1955.

Fraisthorpe Beach: Ringed plovers, turnstones and sanderlings favour this beach, and flocks of golden plovers gather in the adjoining fields in late autumn. Scanning with binoculars now involves no embarrassment; in 1994 Fraisthorpe's status as a naturist beach, the only one in Yorkshire, was scrapped.

Skipsea: A huge flat topped mound was once surmounted by a castle built by Drogo de Bever, a lieutenant of William the Conqueror. The castle was separated from its outer ramparts, also visible, by a tidal mere crossed by a wooden causeway. A collection of shack homes is an intriguing modern sight — much less objectionable than the bungalows and trailer-home parks that blight the cliffs between Filey and Scarborough and around Barmston.

Staithes *Den Oldroyd*

Hornsea: Pop 7,900. Seafront Hornsea's chief attraction is a simple prom next to a gently-sloping mile-long sandy beach.

A pleasant park provides a stroll to Hornsea village, whose trees and several unspoilt cobble-built cottages give it a rustic charm. Lawrence of Arabia was once a guest at White Cottage, Newbegin. The apparent folly of Bettinson's tower, down Willow Drive, was built in 1844 by a Hull businessman to give his servants early sight of his approaching carriage. Woe betide Cook if a hot meal was not ready on the table.

Hornsea Folk Museum: Newbegin. Award winning small museum, mainly designed to show how its former farming occupants lived 100 years ago. Easter-October, Mon-Sat 10-5, Sun 2-5. £1.50, children and Senior citizens £1. Family £4.95. 01964 533443.

Hornsea Pottery: Potters Way. The handthrowing of terracotta pottery is the craft centrepiece of this leisure and retail park. Its other attractions include a Birds of Prey Centre, vintage car collection, and 'Shopping Village,' a highly-popular outlet for end of season stock, especially clothes, by High St. retailers. Daily from 10. Free entry but some charges inside. 01964 534211.

Market Day — Sun, Wed and Bank Holiday. Launched only in 1982 this market, in Sands Lane, has proved so successful that its 100 or so stalls, originally outdoors, are now under a glazed roof. The fishing boats land nearby.

Annual Event: Three-day carnival, mid July. 01964 535257.

Hornsea Mere: Within a mile of the sea, the two-mile long and mile-wide Mere is Yorkshire's largest freshwater lake. Boating and angling takes place in the eastern half, where boats can be hired and sailing tuition is available. The rest of the lake is an important RSPB reserve.

Trees blanched white identify a cormorant roost. Canada, greylag and barnacle geese are other permanent residents, and the reserve is also rich in butterflies, the most vivid being the Red Admiral and orange tip. A footpath beginning near the south shore rises to a bank at the west side, from which there are attractive views. Guided tours — minimum ten people — can be arranged through The Warden, 11, Carlton Avenue, Hornsea, HU18 1JG. 01964 533903.

TIC Newbegin: Easter-late September, daily except Wed and Sun, 9.30-4.30. 01964 536404.

4 NORTHERN DALES

by W. R. Mitchell

(The Howgills, Sedbergh and Dentdale, Garsdale, Wensleydale, including Ripon, and Swaledale).

In the north-west is a wedge of slatey landscape, which has the Howgill Fells as a backdrop. For centuries it belonged to Yorkshire, and councillors attended meetings in distant Wakefield, but when the Boundary Commission played fast-and-loose with the borders in 1974, it became part of the new county of Cumbria. It none the less remains part of the Yorkshire Dales National Park.

Those two exquisite northerly dales — Wensleydale and Swaledale — were switched from the North Riding to the new-fangled North Yorkshire and came under a district council which took on the romantic old name of Richmondshire. It is now much better known as Herriot Country, after James

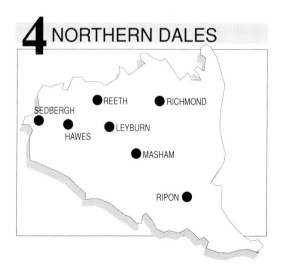

4 NORTHERN DALES

SEDBERGH • REETH • RICHMOND • LEYBURN • HAWES • MASHAM • RIPON •

Herriot, the pen-name of Alf Wight, the vet, who wrote down his Dales experiences in a series of best-selling books.

Herriot became familiar with the Dales while helping a vet who was based on Leyburn. He became fascinated by the hill farmers — "a race apart, proud, independent, spirited." The Herriot haunts, as portrayed at the cinema and in 49 television films, commended the northern Dales to a world-wide audience.

Details of a scenic drive entitled The Herriot Trail, taking in locations from the films, are published at 40p by Richmondshire District Council, Swale House, Frenchgate, Richmond (01748 850222). A copy is available at local information centres.

The Howgills: These slatey, grassy, wall-less comparatively little-known hills, which are named after an obscure hamlet on the Lune Valley side, have their own appeal and shadow pattern. Someone compared their rounded forms with those of a herd of elephants which had lain down to sleep.

The grandest edge of the Howgills is Cautley Crag (seen from the road between Sedbergh and Kirkby Stephen). Cautley Spout is actually a series of waterfalls with a total fall of 700 ft. A footpath leading beside it is a popular way to the highest point of the Howgills (the Calf).

Sedbergh: Huddling against Winder, the town bears a name which is said to mean "flat-topped hill". It has the appearance of a small Victorian town, and High Victorianism is apparent at the chapel and some of the imposing houses of Sedbergh School, founded by Roger Lupton in the 16th century.

Sedbergh parish church does not look especially old yet has Norman origins. A small tract of land nearby is the setting for a few market stalls on Wednesday, but the main market is on ground at the eastern side of the main street, which takes one-way traffic. The market charter dates from 1251. Early closing day is Thursday.

In Finkle Street, just across the road from the church is Hollett's antiquarian bookshop, always good for a browse. One of its specialities is books about the North Country. (015396 20298).

The town is associated with the early days of Quakerism. George Fox, a frequent visitor, preached by an outcrop of rock above Firbank (a rock still known as Fox's Pulpit). Two miles down Lunesdale from Sedbergh is the Friends' Meeting House of Brigflatts (1675). Those who gather there have around them many original fitments and furnishings.

National Park Centre (015396 20125).

Dentdale: Dent Town has retained its cobbles in the main street. On reaching them, the teeth of unsuspecting motorists chatter like castanets. The village (for such it is) has a capacious car park. A coffin-like slab of Shap granite, propped against a building in the main street, is a memorial to Adam Sedgwick (1785-1873), one of the fathers of modern geology, who was born locally.

St. Andrew's Church has Jacobean box pews and memorials made of Dent Marble, a form of limestone, once quarried in the gills of the upper dale. The stone is dark, adorned by white or grey fossils.

Southey wrote of "the terrible knitters 'e Dent". The word 'terrible' as used here, means "great", relat-

Dent   *T. A. Edwards*

ing to their energy and skill. Wool delivered weekly from Kendal was distributed among the knitters who, when the next delivery was made, handed over the stockings, gloves and other goods they had knitted. You'll hear a lot about hand-knitting at Dent.

Dent Brewery (01539 625326), built in 1990, uses spring water from Rise Hill and supplies an increasing number of Dales pubs with traditional ales. Dent railway station, which is several miles from Dent itself, and some 600 ft higher than the valley floor, is part of the Settle-Carlisle Railway and at 1,150 ft, the highest mainline station in Britain.

Garsdale: This open-ended, ten mile long valley, drained by the River Clough, is well patronised by travellers for, with Wensleydale, the A684 provides a low level east-west route through the otherwise unfriendly Pennines.

Garsdale is hemmed in by Baugh Fell (north) and Rise Hill (south). The main settlement (known as The Street) has two places of worship — a stylish church and a diminutive chapel. Judging by many of the buildings, especially farms, the 17th century was a prosperous time for Garsdale.

Inquire about a leaflet, issued by the National Park authority, on the two mile long Sedgwick Geological

Sheep sale at Tan Hill   *W. R. Mitchell*

Trail at Garsdale Foot.

At the head of Garsdale is a former railway junction (Settle-Carlisle and the Wensleydale line). Also near the head of the valley is secluded Grisedale, which (in a popular book) was described as "The Dale that Died." A tiny Methodist chapel standing near the viaduct crossing the A684 is said to have been built with the help of Settle-Carlisle navvies.

WENSLEYDALE

Broad and pastoral, and edged by tabular hills, Wensleydale looks more sylvan than the other dales. Wensleydale cheese has given its name a wide recognition.Wensleydale cheese was originally made from the milk of sheep, not cows.

Wensleydale takes its name from a once-thriving village near Leyburn. The river is Ure and an old name for the dale is Yoredale. (The Yoredale Series of rocks, alternating bands of limestones, shales and grits, were so named by the geologist Phillips, who made a special study of the strata at the head of Wensleydale).

The Moorcock Inn at 1,063ft is marked on many a map of England because of its solitary position at the junction of the A684 with the Mallerstang road (B 6269), leading to Kirkby Stephen.

Hawes: This dalehead market town is little more than two lines of shops, houses and businesses and therefore resembles a mid-West town, minus the hitching posts. It is extremely busy on a Tuesday (market day) and throughout the holiday season. Early closing is on Wednesday. The market rights were awarded as recently as 1700.

Hawes (originally named Le Thouse, a pass through the hills) was for centuries an obscure spot in the Forest of Wensleydale. With an increase in packhorse traffic and the re-routing of the Lancaster-Richmond turnpike, it became a busy little place. The churches of Hawes and Hardraw are the only ones which stand beside the Pennine Way footpath.

There is free entertainment in watching farmers

buy or sell stock at Hawes's busy auction mart. In October, the time of the big sheep sales, Hawes heaves with farmers.

It has a Town Trail (ask locally for a leaflet) and, conscious of the importance of tourism to the local economy has blossomed into a major interpretation centre for the Dales way of life.

Dales Countryside Museum in Station Yard (01969 667494). The exhibits, based on a nucleus of Dales byegones given by Marie Hartley and Joan Ingilby, now range across 10,000 years of local activity from the end of the Ice Age. A Local Studies Centre is being developed.

Ropeworks which for years traded under the name of W. R. Outhwaite and Son is now run by Peter and Ruth Annison (01969 667487). Visitors are welcome. Admission is free. Outhwaites make church bell ropes, bannister and barrier ropes, clothes lines, skipping ropes and dog leads. The ropeworks are closed on Saturdays from November to June and on Sundays throughout the year.

Wensleydale Creamery, in Gayle Road (01969 667664), threatened with closure but then the subject of a management buy-out, has blossomed as never before. Apart from the basic activity of producing Wensleydale cheese, there is now a visitor centre, complete with a special video film detailing the stages of cheese-making; a viewing gallery, specialist cheese shop and a restaurant, with ample parking.

National Park Centre for information (01969 667450).

Hardraw: Pass through the Green Dragon Hotel to enter a short, deep little valley ending in Hardraw Scar, over which pours Hardraw Force, the highest unbroken waterfall in Yorkshire (96ft). At times it looks like a shimmering grey curtain; at others it is as though a tap has been turned full-on, and yet again (in the coldest winter) it is like a monstrous icicle. Hardy visitors may walk behind the fall. But take care on the wet rocks.

An annual event is a brass band contest, with the

Hardraw Force   *Clifford Robinson*

musicians playing on a special bandstand lower down the valley. It is said to have excellent acoustics.

At Hardraw, the Pennine Way continues its stern course northwards over Great Shunner Fell — remote, bleak, peaty — at 2,340ft. Walking to the summit and back is a good outing on a clear day, when the table-tops of the Wensleydale hills and (westwards) Ingleborough are clear to see.

Bainbridge: On Brough Hill, a grassy eminence above the River Bain, the Romans had one of the forts from which (on good roads) they policed the territory of the Brigantes (and protected their lead-mining interests!). The Romans were here for three centuries.

Happy is the village with a green. Bainbridge's is huge and rectangular, complete with stocks. The moaning sound of the forest horn is heard at the Green between September 27 (Holyrood) and Shrovetide. At other times, the horn is kept in the Rose and Crown Hotel. Bainbridge is named after a crossing point of the River Bain, which, at two miles, is claimed to be England's shortest river. This is the outflow of Semerwater, a lake immortalised in verse as the site of a city which was consigned to a watery grave because of its inhospitality to a visiting beggar:

Semerwater rise, Semerwater sink
And swallow all the town,
Save yon little house
Where they gave me food and drink.

Semerwater is a glacial lake subject to flash floods, one of which probably overwhelmed a small lake settlement of prehistoric times. The folk memory has come to us in an embroidered form down many centuries.

It is a resort of water-skiers in summer (01969 650436). They stop for an hour on a Sunday in August for an open-air service, when the vicar is carried to a boat, which he uses as a pulpit, and Hawes brass band (on the shore) accompanies the hymn-singing.

Askrigg: An elegant village, with a spacious 15th century parish church and many, linked three-storey buildings, including Cringley House, the facade of which was used as "Skeldale House" in the BBC's James Herriot series. A scenic road from Askrigg climbs to the moors and then descends to Swaledale, which is reached near Gunnerside.

Bolton Castle   *Bertram Unne*

Aysgarth: Down the hill, by the River Ure, the water creams as it tumbles over horizontal beds of rock, creating three groups of cascades. The Upper Falls, most familiar, are viewed from a single span bridge, widened in 1788, which seems like a rainbow set in stone.

Most visitors park their cars (and pay a charge) beside the National Park Centre (approached from either Aysgarth or near Carperby, on the other side of the dale). The walk to the Upper Falls is easy. Yore Mill, an 18th century structure which houses the Yorkshire Carriage Museum, includes among its diverse exhibits a Brougham, "still haunted by the ghost of a Scottish gardener".

A footpath from the National Park Centre, through Freeholders' Wood, leads to the Middle Falls (good view of St. Andrew's church, across the river) and the Lower Aysgarth Falls.

West Burton, near Aysgarth, is approached via a one-way traffic system and groups itself around a green where horses are often tethered. West Burton thrived with lead-mining and quarrying, but not a whiff of industry apart from farming is detectable today.

The village is the place from which to explore a delightful cul de sac dale, Walden, which ends with a big sheep farm called — Kentucky! West Burton lies just off the B 6160, an attractive route up Bishopdale, one of the deepest of the Yorkshire dales. Kidstones Pass leads the traveller to Upper Wharfedale.

West Witton: A drawn-out village which springs to maximum life in August when Bartle (effigy of a sheep-stealer) is ritualistically burnt. At the same time, those officiating recite an old chant about the punishment meted out to Bartle. It's excitingly barbaric.

Castle Bolton: You can see the castle from afar. It is perched high on a hillside some six miles from Leyburn with an attendant church and two rows of modest cottages extending away.

Fred Lawson, a Dales artist of note, who lived at the eastern end of the village, commended it to a host of people through his pictures.

Castle Bolton was built in 1379 by Richard Scrope (pronounced Scroop), who paid the enormous sum of £12,000 for the work. It was not intended to be a castle in the old sense; more a well-constructed apartment block, with walls thick enough to deter raiders. Mary Queen of Scots was held prisoner at Castle Bolton from July 1567 to January 1569. Open daily from March to November, 10am to 5pm. Refreshments and shop. (Tel: 0969 23981).

Wensley: Here are the main gates to Bolton Hall, the mansion home of Lord Bolton. The village after which the dale was named is of modest size, but attractive, and having a historic, 13th century church incorporating a screen from Easby Abbey and splendidly ornate pews for my lord of the manor. The church was used by the BBC when filming the wedding of James Herriot and his bride in the television series.

In the churchyard are the graves of Peter Goldsmith, surgeon on HMS Victory, who held in his arms the dying Nelson at the Battle of Trafalgar, and the comedian Al Read.

Leyburn: The name of this market town which has an influence throughout Wensleydale is said to be derived from "Le borne", or a stream by a clearing. The first impression is of a vast market place, surrounded by shops, some of which are splendidly old-fashioned (early 19th century).

Apart from the main dale road, a good route crosses high ground to Grinton in Swaledale and another is a comparatively fast route to Richmond.

The market hall is of Regency style (though dates from well within the Victorian period).

Leyburn has developed its tourist interests and facilities include caravan parks. Visitors enjoy a comparatively short walk from town to the Shawl, a limestone escarpment with trees which, although less than 100 ft in elevation, affords a panoramic view of Wensleydale.

Shops: Good range of traditional shops. Market

Middleham Castle

Day, Friday; early closing Wednesday. Swineside Ceramics (novelty teapots) is at The Teapottery, Leyburn (01969 23839). Dalesmade Centre in association with Tana Stained Glass at 7 Railway Street (01969 24312). Tennant's Auction Centre is a popular attraction (01969 23780).

Tourist information (01969 23069/22773).

Constable Burton Gardens: Just off the A684 east of Leyburn. Gardens associated with a John Carr house (1768). Alpines, rockeries, roses and shrubs. Woodland walk. Lake. (01677 50428).

Middleham: Two miles from Leyburn, and across the river (using an iron girder bridge built by public subscription) is Middleham, where one of the dominant sounds is the clip-clop of racehorse hooves as strings of horses — some of the 200 or so kept locally — go to and from the moorland exercise grounds.

Racing stables have been a feature of the town for two centuries. Long before this, Middleham was renowned for its 12th century castle. The blocky Norman keep casts a shadow over attractive houses and squares in a town which has the friendly character of a village.

Historically, Middleham's great days were during the War of the Roses, when the Duke of Gloucester (who became Richard III) joined the household of the Earl of Warwick to be tutored. He wooed and wed Anne, the Earl's daughter (1472). It was while they were living at Middleham that Anne gave birth to Edward, their only son (1473).

Richard was crowned King of England in 1483. Then came the years of sorrow. Within a year, their son was dead (Richard made a trip north on hearing the news). Anne died not long afterwards. Richard was slain at Bosworth (1485). Middleham Castle is "open to view" (01969 23899).

Opposite the Castle is the workshop of the sculpture Peter Hibbard, who produces carvings in stone or wood. Arrangements can be made for studio visits, demonstrations or courses. Shop open 10am to 5pm daily, except for off-season Tuesdays. (01969 23056).

The church is dedicated to St. Alkelda. Only one other church has this saint as patron, and that is Giggleswick. It is said that Alkelda, a "Saxon princess", was strangled by heathen women while on a journey between the two places. Each church has a stained glass reproduction of the throttling. (Some people think Alkelda was a Christianisation of the spirit of local wells.)

Market Day: Sunday, in summer only.

Jervaulx Abbey: The remains of the 12th century Abbey (where, some believe, the original Wensleydale cheese was made) may be visited at times specified on the roadside noticeboard. Of special interest are the remains of chapter house and dormitory. A small roadside car park is available. (01677 60226).

At High Jervaulx Farm, Brymor Ice Cream is made. The Ice Cream parlour, on the farm, is open to visitors. Thirty flavours of ice cream are on display. Open all year, 10am to 6pm. (01677 460377).

Masham: The great days of Masham market were in the 18th and 19th centuries when, in mid-September, there might be 70,000 sheep and lambs at a special fair. Now the town is famous for its Steam Engine and Fair Organ Rally (July).

St. Mary's Church, characterised by some Norman work and octagonal bell-stage, plus a spire, has an adjacent 9th century stone cross.

In the Market Place are the premises of Uredale Glass, makers of handmade coloured crystal glassware, vases, etc. Nominal charge for demonstration. Open Easter-Oct 31, 10am to 5pm. Nov-Easter, Tues to Sat. (01765 689780).

Jervaulx Abbey *D. A. Marsh*

Masham is renowned for Theakston's brewery (which dates back to the 1820s) and for the potent "Old Peculier" (a reference to Masham's Peculier Court, a powerful ecclesiastical body). Theakston's have a visitor centre, with video presentations and many objects of reference to Masham and its brewery. There are conducted tours and ale-tasting. (01765 689057).

Black Sheep, a newly-established brewery, is owned by Paul Theakston, fifth generation of Masham's famous brewing family. Tours available through a booking system. Daytime, 4 pm. Evening, groups only, 7-30pm except Friday. Shop open on weekdays. (01765 689227).

Ask in Masham for directions to Ilton and the mock Druid's Temple, built by a local landowner on an airy ridge but now surrounded by the conifers of Jervaulx Forest. Here is a picnic site, car park and (not very far away) the fascinating assembly of stones, each one named. At the end of the complex is a mysterious little cave.

Lightwater Valley: At North Stainley, three and a-half miles north of Ripon, this is a 125 acre country theme park. In addition to thrills provided by The Ultimate, the world's largest roller-coaster, The Soopa Loopa, The Rat and The Wave are more leisurely rides on water or rail. Self-service restaurant and coffee shop. Picnic areas. Open: Saturday, Mar 26-Oct 31; daily in June, July, August only. 24 hour hotline: (01765 635368).

Thorp Perrow Arboretum: This outstanding collection of trees and shrubs is to be found two and a-half miles south of Bedale on the Well to Ripon road. (01677 425323).

Over 1,000 species are set in 85 acres. In spring, a display of flowers reared from bulbs. In summer, wild flowers are profuse. In autumn, the tints of trees and shrubs are breathtaking. Features of tourist interest include children's mystery trail, nature trail, picnic area and a tearoom information centre. Large space for parking. Open: daily (dawn to dusk) throughout

Aysgarth Lower Falls   *Robert Rixon*

the year. (0677) 425323).

Ripon: This historic city received its Charter of Incorporation from Alfred the Great (886 AD). Its Cathedral evolved from a simple church (655), which later came under the patronage of St. Wilfrid. Within the building is the oldest complete Anglo-Saxon crypt in England (672), the dimensions being traditionally the same as those of the tomb in which Jesus was laid.

The newest Cathedral treasury (a feature opened in 1988) contains the largest collections of silver and silver gilt ecclesiastical treasures in the land. No charge for admission to the cathedral is made, but a donation of £1.50 a head is invited. (01765 604108).

The enormous market place at Ripon has, as its centrepiece, an Obelisk (successor to the market cross, in 1781). On Market Day (Thursday) it is surrounded by stalls. Daily, at 9pm, the Ripon Hornblower blows his horn while standing at each corner of the Obelisk to "set the watch", as it has been for over 1,100 years.

At the edge of the market place is the Wakeman's House, the title of the worthy who was appointed chief magistrate. The last Wakeman and first Mayor of Ripon was Hugh Ripley, who died in 1637. The

Swaledale, looking past Thwaite towards Muker
I. Holmes

House now contains a museum.

Events: Two-week Ripon Charter Festival, late May/early June. St. Wilfrid's Procession, last Saturday in July (01765 604579).

Sports: Spa Gardens offer bowls or pitch and putt. Refreshments.

Museum: Police and Prison, St. Mary's Gate (01765 690799). The building began as a House of Correction in 1686. The museum, in a cell block, has displays and exhibits illustrating the maintenance of law and order locally since the 10th century.

Tourist information (01765 604625).

Newby Hall: Dates back to 1690s, when it was the home of Sir Edward Blackett. Re-designed in the 18th century by Robert Adam. Twenty-five acres of garden. Restaurant. Daily, Apr-Sept except Mondays (but including Bank Holidays). From 11am. (01423 322583).

Swaledale: Just 22 miles long, from Keld to Richmond, the upper dale has a remote feel and the Norse flavour is detectable after 1,000 years. The principal settlements — Keld, Thwaite, Muker, Gunnerside — are Norse. Their spirit was held in the manner and speech of the old-time dalesfolk.

The Swale rises in a wilderness of acid moors, tufty with ling, and mosses where cotton grass has been the main peat-forming plant. The side valleys and much of the upper ground has been disturbed by miners seeking galena (lead ore) and on Tan Hill are the remains of drift mines for the thin, brittle coal of the Yoredale Series of rocks. All this delights those with a taste for history.

Mr Wainwright's Coast to Coast Walk (coming down from Nine Standards Rigg) and the Pennine Way are two notable local footpaths, each followed by thousands of walkers per year. Raven Seat, near the dalehead, is typical of the big sheep farms of the area.

Keld and Tan Hill: The short, sharp Norse name means "spring". This is an area of tumbling and rushing water. The Swale itself, fresh from Wainwath Falls, in the shadow of a range of limestone cliffs, is soon flowing "back o' Kisdon", an island-hill, capped with heather and with its own little colony of red grouse.

Near Keld, a road zig-zags up to West Stonesdale and then settles down for a steady climb to the top of Tan Hill, where — after four miles — a solitary inn (especially welcome to perspiring Pennine Wayfarers) breaks the skyline.

Keld has a youth hostel. There is also a farmhouse at which cups of tea are available. Coast to Coasters remember every delicious mouthful.

Thwaite: A cottage with a decorated lintel above the main doorway, featuring birds and beasts, is the birthplace of Richard and Cherry Kearton. The brothers were born in 1862 and 1871 respectively. Richard died at his home in Surrey in 1928 and Cherry lived on to 1940.

These sons of a shepherd had left their native dale for London and they achieved fame as pioneers of wildlife photography, taking advantage of the new American half-tone system of illustration to produce natural history books with "real photographs". Cherry spent many years in Africa, where he photographed big game and befriended apes, recording his adventures in many books. The Kearton Guest House is renowned for its meals.

Muker: This is a place from which to climb Kisdon, from the beckside to a breezy little tract of moorland at an elevation atop 1,600 ft. At Muker, you see a moorland beck. The Swale has shyly slipped behind Kisdon.

The church was built in the 16th century and much "improved" in the 18th and 19th centuries. Prior to the consecration of a churchyard, those who died were borne — at great cost of time and energy — to the nearest consecrated ground at Grinton. The route became known as the Corpse Road.

Muker Show sees the village packed with folk and Muker's celebrated brass band (established, 1879) in good form.

Gunnerside: From the B6270, before the river is crossed on a downdale journey, a first view of Gunnerside reveals a stonescape, created by wallers, lead-miners and builders.

Gunnerside was a lead-mining village, populous enough for an enormous Methodist chapel to be built. Gunnerside Gill, some four miles long, is worth exploring, especially in spring, the flowers include spring sandwort (a plant tolerant of lead which abounds in an area) and yellow mountain pansy, sometimes with purple patches, this hybrid known to one botanist as "Mickey Mouse pansies".

Arkengarthdale: From Low Road, a road crosses a ridge to Langthwaite in Arkengarthdale. Where the road dips at Surrender Mill, it is sometimes possible to find a parking place for the car and to walk up the little valley to examine the remains of Old Gang Mines. On a nearby hill-edge are two gable-ends and

Frenchgate, Richmond   *Michael Dobson*

lines of stone pillars (all that remains of a smelters' peat store).

The road to Arkengarthdale reaches that valley near the CB Hotel. The initials are of Charles Bathhurst, who bought the local manor in 1656 and developed lead-mining.

Reeth: Now very touristy, was once an important centre, with a population of 1,300. Its interests included lead mining, farming and the hand-knitting of stockings and gloves which gave most people (not just women) a lucrative sideline. At the peak of its development, Reeth had seven fairs and a market (Friday).

The old Methodist schoolroom houses a folk museum Open daily, from Easter to October, 10-30am to 5-30pm, and there is an admission charge.

Stef's Models (workshop and shop) features animal sculptures and models designed by Stef Ottevanger (01748 884498).

Richmond: The nucleus is a Norman "new town". The castle was being built in 1071 at the instructions of Alan Rufus, who selected the natural spot — the top of a cliff overlooking the River Swale. The Norman keep of Richmond Castle, one of the finest in the land, is 100ft high (01748 822493).

A modest stroll around Castle Walk reveals the town in its dramatic setting above the Swale. Among the attractive riverside walks is one (taking about half an hour) to Easby Abbey. Upstream lies Round Howe (woodland).

A vast cobbled Square, with Trinity Church within and Georgian-style houses around, are seen by those who have energetically climbed to the top of the keep. In Frenchgate lived Frances I'anson, the "Sweet Lass of Richmond Hill".

Shopping: Variety of shops, which tend to stay open in summer. Market Day is Saturday. Indoor market on Thursday and Friday. Early closing: Wednesday.

Entertainments: Georgian Theatre Royal, built in 1788 by Samuel Butler, actor/manager, and restored to its original appearance in 1963. It is the oldest theatre in Britain which survives in its original form. Theatre Museum contains playbills and complete set of painted scenery (dating from 1836). Guided tours, April-October. Gift shop. (01748 823710). In June, a Richmond Folk Festival takes place (01748 825487).

Museums: Richmondshire Museum, Ryder's Wynd, includes local history and the BBC's reconstruction of a vet's surgery, as used in the Herriot television series. Group guided tours by arrangement. Shop. Open daily, Good Friday to end of October, 11am-5pm. Other times by appointment. Admission charge. Party rates available (01748 825611).

The Green Howards Museum, featuring over 300 years of regimental history and an impressive array of silver. Trinity Church Square (01748 822133). Open daily, Apr-Oct, 9-30am — 4-30pm. (Sun, 2pm to 4-30pm). Inquire about openings at other times of the year. The museum is closed in December and January. Admission charge.

Tourist information (01749 850252 or 825994).

5 SOUTHERN DALES

by W. R. Mitchell

(Malhamdale, Wharfedale, Littondale, Nidderdale (incorporating Harrogate and Knaresborough) and The Three Peaks countryside.

Of the 600 dales in Yorkshire, the most dramatic and best-known are grouped in the north-west of Yorkshire, where 680 square miles of the most delectable country were designated the Yorkshire Dales National Park (notice the roadside signs featuring the head of a Swaledale tup — a male sheep of the native breed).

"The Dales" has become a general name for the region north of the Aire Gap (which the romantic thinks of as a missing link in the Pennine Chain). Between the well-known valleys, up which 95 per cent of the visitors drive, are vast tracts of little-known sheep-cropped fells and heather moors.

In the south-west of the National Park is the largest outcrop of limestone in Britain, from which rise the Three Peaks (Whernside, Ingleborough, Penyghent), each over 2,000 ft high.

The upper dales are linked by roads which cross some of the least-spoilt fell country in England and

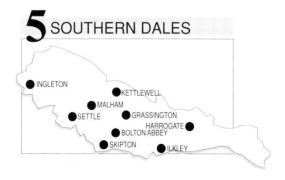

enable motorists to go mountaineering. Good examples are the Buttertubs Pass which extends from Hardraw (Wensleydale) to near Thwaite (Swaledale), and the Silverdale road from Stainforth in Ribblesdale to Halton Gill, at the head of Littondale, extending back o' Penyghent.

The beauty of the Dales is more than skin-deep. In the Limestone Country, 1,000 cave and pothole systems excite specialist explorers (potholers). Several well-lit "show" caves are available for the holiday-maker.

Skipton: Population 13,583. The name of this old market town beside Eller Beck, a tributary of the Aire, means "sheep town". It is the capital of the vaguely defined district known as Craven and was the crowded gateway to the Yorkshire Dales until a system of by-passes was initiated.

The best-known features are a broad High Street, leading the eye to ancient castle and large church. Progress along the High Street on market day is relatively slow, but not without interest. Many of the spooky little yards which characterised Old Skipton vanished in a mania for development.

The Castle is everything a visitor would expect — a medieval structure, perched on a sheer rock on one side and having a gateway with castellated drum towers on the other. (To see the awesome side of the Castle, follow the towpath of the Springs Canal from Mill Bridge).

Skipton Castle is fully roofed and proudly flies the check flag of the Clifford family, who settled here in the 14th century and, after the place had been knocked about a bit during the Civil War, restored it. The restorer, Lady Anne Clifford (born at Skipton in 1590 and the last of the family using that name) was almost a queen in the northern dales.

Visitors use a gateway set between the massive drum towers. Cut in stone is the Clifford family motto: DESORMAIS (Henceforth). Open daily (except on Christmas Day) from 10am; on Sunday, 2pm. New shop (01756 792442).

Lady Anne also restored Holy Trinity Church (which had been founded in the 14th century) and the initials AP (Anne Pembroke) in stained glass form a diamond pane on one of the windows. A magnificent roof and tombs of some of the proud and fabulous Cliffords, flank the altar. The oaken screen, of 16th century date, is said to have come from Bolton Priory.

Skipton was changed by the arrival of the Leeds and Liverpool Canal and its branch, Springs Canal, along which was conveyed stone from a large quarry. Today, there's a profusion of brightly-painted private boats. Pennine Boat Trips offer canal cruising (01756 790829). Pennine Cruisers hire out boats (01756 795478).

Shopping: The town, with three market days a week, suits the shopaholic. Craven Court has been devised as a Victorian style shopping arcade.

Transport: A59 is the principal west-east route with

Canal at Skipton   *Den Oldroyd*

East Marton, near Skipton   *Clifford Robinson*

the A65 (Keighley-Kendal) a somewhat narrow and winding road extending north from Skipton. It's not worth overtaking. Bus links with Ilkley, Keighley, Barnoldswick, Settle and Malham. BR station links the town with Leeds and (northwards, on the fabulous Settle-Carlisle) with Appleby and Carlisle.

Entertainment: Plaza Cinema and Video Entertainment Complex, Sackville Street (01756 793417).

Sport: Aireville Park Leisure — swimming, tennis, putting green. (01756 792805). Coulthurst Craven Sports Centre, Sandylands (01756 795181).

Museum: Craven Museum, Town Hall. Archaeology, social history, farming, geology and local history. Open Mon, Wed-Fri., 11am to 5pm, Sun 2pm to 5pm. Admission free. Tourist Information: (01756 792809).

Malhamdale: Follow the A65 from Skipton to Gargrave or Coniston Cold, and turn right for Malhamdale. The river (formed of two mountain becks half a mile below Malham village) is the Aire.

To reach Malham you pass through Airton to Kirkby Malham. As the name implies, this is where the Anglican church stands — a 15th century church known, from its size and grandeur, as the Minster of the Dales. Handy car parking. Stroll down the road to the Aire bridge at Hanlith. and riverside footpaths.

Beyond Kirkby Malham, the view opens up to reveal Malham Cove (finest headpiece of any dale, being a cliff of gleaming limestone the height of which is variously estimated in books from 230 to 300ft. The average will not be far out).

Nearby is Gordale Scar, another of the "gee whiz" features, a gorge with overhanging cliffs 300ft high. In the high season (which stretches from January to December) don't be tempted to take a car along the road to Gordale. Walk on the good path to Janet's Foss (a fan-shaped waterfall in a sheltered and floriferous little ravine) and then continue a short distance to the path leading into Gordale, which is not a collapsed cave, as many suppose, but was carved out by a furious rush of melt-water from the glacial ice. Among the old-time gawpers were William and Dorothy Wordsworth.

Malham, one of the Dales "honeypots", has a National Park Centre (01729 830363) complete with capacious park which is usually oversubscribed at weekends. There are two old inns, a few shops and the Cove Centre, incorporating a sales area for outdoor clothes and equipment, a craft workshop and buttery (01729 830432).

Most visitors walk to Malham Cove, and the toughest make a knee-cracking ascent of a wooden-framed stairway leads to the limestone pavement above the Cove. The grey weathered limestone looks like the lobes of a brain. Blocks of limestone are "clints" and the gaps in between the blocks are "grykes".

Roads from the village pass on either side of the cove to reach Malham Moor and Malham Tarn. On the moor is a preserved chimney relating to the smelting of galena (lead ore) and later the roasting of local calamine (zinc ore used for brass-making).

A parking space for cars lies within easy walking distance of the outflow of Malham Tarn. There may also be an ice cream van. The track to Malham Tarn House is for authorised vehicles only, but may be used as a footpath.The Tarn (1,230ft) is the centre of a 4,200 acre site owned by the National Trust. It rests on a saucer-shaped bed of Silurian Slate in what is otherwise a limestone countryside where water speedily drains away down cracks and crannies.

Malham Tarn has been declared a wetland of international importance. and home to some 19 species of nationally rare plants. The National Trust has a head warden/naturalist, based at Waterhouses (01729 830416) and the area is managed as a nature reserve by the Field Studies Council, based at Tarn House (01729 830331), from whom day-tickets for anglers (including the hire of a boat) are available.

Wharfedale: Anyone who drives up Wharfedale is never far from the river. At first, there is a choice of roads; then a single highway (B6160) heads for the river's source at Beckermonds.

Wharfedale has been quite well populated since the 6th century, when Anglian settlers claimed the best land and established the nuclei of the villages seen today. At the dale head, the dour Norse settlers farmed a grudging landscape.

The river remains clear and cool, a resort of dippers and grey wagtails, for angling interests have been strong and water is abstracted from reservoirs and the river to meet the needs of thirsty cities.

Ilkley, the town standing where Wharfedale begins to feel like a dale, spreads itself comfortably along the lower slopes of gritstone moors. The dominant rock is brown. At Bolton Abbey, the eye ranges across heathered moors. Further up the dale, beyond the tumultuous rush of water known as the Strid and melancholic remains of Barden Tower (an old hunting lodge) the limestone is evident.

Pearl-white scars overlook the Wharfe at Burnsall. The sphinx-like form of Kilnsey Crag dominates the area where Wharfedale is joined by Littondale (at Amerdale Dub).

Upper Wharfedale has gathered about itself many fabulous stories. The area breathes romance. Most tales are best told in the evening, when critical facilities are none too sharp. Did fairies really dance at Elbolton, one of the celebrated reef-knolls (which were colourful and alive in a shallow sea millions of years ago)? The author Halliwell Sutcliffe, a great manufacturer of romantic tales, filled the little hamlet of Thorpe, near Grassington, with energetic cobblers.

Ilkley: Population 13,530. Cow and Calf Rocks at edge of Ilkley Moor are of gritstone, the Cow having a rock face 50ft high which has a strong appeal to climbers.

Prehistoric man, intensely superstitious, carved many cup-and-ring marks (also a swastika, ancient good luck symbol) on moorland outcrops. The Swastika Stone, near Hebers Ghyll a wooden ravine with bridges, is believed to be the oldest rock carving in Yorkshire.

The Romans, building a road through the Aire Gap and on to York, established a fort at Olicana their name for Ilkley in AD 79. The site of the fort is where the Manor House now stands. The Grove, a swell

Cow and Calf rocks, Ilkley　　　　　　　　　　*Bill Pates*

shopping street, follows the line of a Roman road.

At Ilkley parish church are The Saxon Crosses, dating back to the Dark Ages. A grammar school was established in 1637 and the Wharfe was bridged in stone in 1673.

The village remained small until the mid-18th century, when Squire Middleton created two open-air spa baths at White Wells. In the 1860s, Bradford woolmen were building mini-mansions at Ilkley and the Victorian character of the town was established. Ilkley's reputation as a spa town led to the opening of no less than 15 hydros.

A visiting choir from Halifax are said to have made up the famous song "Ilkla' Moor". The 84-mile Dales Way from Ilkley to Windermere starts at the Old Bridge.

Shopping: Gracious town-centre streets include Brook Street and The Grove. Moors Shopping Centre and a major development next to Ilkley railway station. Handy car parks. Early closing: Wednesday.

Transport: Good bus service to Skipton, Bradford and Leeds. Trains to Leeds.

Entertainment: Kings Hall and Winter Gardens, Station Road (01943 607168). Ilkley Playhouse, Weston Road (eight productions, Sept-July — 0943

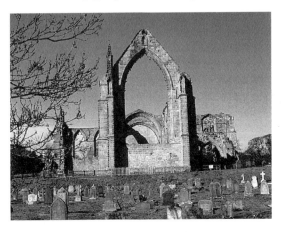

Bolton Priory

Rock climbing at Almscliffe Crags, near Harrogate

609539).

Sports: The Lawn Tennis Club (01943 607182). Swimming, open air pool and indoor five-lane pool. Daily in summer; closed Fridays in winter (01943 600453). Golf, 18 holes (01943 607277). Lido, with sunbathing and picnic lawns (May-September). Crown Green bowls and putting. Rowing on River Wharfe (cafe bar).

Events: Literature Festival. Authors and books. (01943 601210). Yorkshire Artists' and British Watercolour Society Exhibition (twice yearly at The King's Hall). Wharfedale Musical Festival, competitive (two weeks before Spring Bank Holiday).

Places of Interest: The Manor House, Castle Yard, has a splendid 17th century king-post roof. Museum and Art Gallery features furniture of yeoman farmer's house, 17th and 18th centuries. Open Tues-Sun and Bank Holiday Mondays. Closed Good Friday, Christmas Day, Boxing Day. (01943 600066).

White Wells, at the edge of Ilkley Moor, is an 18th century bathhouse extended by a hydropathic company in 1865. Open on Saturdays and Sundays (10am to 5pm). Entry free.

Tourist Information: Station Road (01943 602319).

Embsay Steam Railway: Embsay lies off the Skipton-Bolton Abbey road. The preserved railway runs passenger services, and has its headquarters at the old station in a well-marked position near the centre of the village.

The Steam Railway hopes to have tracks laid to Bolton Abbey by the end of 1994. Meanwhile, steam trains operate regularly on its two and a-half miles of track to Stoneacre Loop. General inquiries: (01756) 794727. Talking timetable: (01756) 795189.

Bolton Abbey: This has been a recognisable estate for 1,000 years and is owned by the Trustees of the Chatsworth Settlement. The name Bolton Abbey, though used for many years, is inappropriate, for here stood an Augustinian Priory.

One of the Dales honeypots, it has a full range of facilities in a park-like setting such as attracted early English painters (Girtin, Cotman, Turner). Large car park in the village (keep your ticket; it admits you to other parks).

An easy walk leads through the hole in the wall to a ruined priory, the nave of which is complete and used as the parish church. The old priory gateway became the nucleus of Bolton Hall, the residence (when in Yorkshire) of the Duke and Duchess of Devonshire.

The Duchess has been prominently associated with the evolution into an outstanding hotel of The Devonshire Arms (not far from the old river bridge, now by-passed). Many paintings from Chatsworth, the family home in Derbyshire, adorn the walls.

The Cavendish Pavilion, approached along a road

Burnsall   *Stanley Bond*

which begins near a big and stylish memorial to a Duke who was assassinated in Ireland, incorporates a restaurant and cafe (01756 710245), with riverbank parking space.

The Pavilion is at the southern entrance to the Strid Woods, where colour-coded paths pass through mature woodland. The paths were laid out by the Rev William Carr (1789-1843) and were commended by Wordsworth. At the Strid (approached from its own special car park) the river swirls and bubbles between outcrops of dark rock. Keep well away from the edge. An old couplet declares:

Wharfe is clear, and Aire is lyth,
Where the Aire drowns one, Wharfe drowns five.

Footpath to Barden Bridge. Up the hill are the remains of Barden Tower. Nearby, a tearoom and also a barn used as a bunkhouse (01756 710533).

Visitor information at Bolton Abbey: 0756 710533. Bolton Abbey Holiday Consortium: 0756 793371.

The Old Cottage, Appletreewick   James P. Gibson

Burnsall: A village with a semi-green (part of it is occupied by a car park). Local people think kindly of Sir William Craven, a native of Aptrick (Appletreewick), across the dale, who moved to London and became Lord Mayor (1610-1612). Not surprisingly, he was called the "Dick Whittington of the Dales". He endowed a grammar school in 1602 (the building, near the church, is now a primary school) and he covered the cost of giving Burnsall one of the most substantial bridges in the Dales.

Appletreewick: Two miles from Burnsall, and situated on the east side of the dale, Appletreewick (referred to locally as Aptrick) was once owned by Bolton Priory, the monks raising sheep and mining lead on the moors. Monks Hall, one of the venerable buildings, was one of the Bolton farms.

The influence of William Craven is to be seen here in the High Hall, a building of Tudor style, which he restored.

At Skyreholme, two miles from Appletreewick, stands Parcevall Hall, which is leased to Bradford Diocese as a retreat and conference centre. The exquisite hall was created from an unpretentious farmhouse in the 1920s by Sir William Milner, a York architect.

Parcevall Hall Gardens, a woodland garden with outstanding views of dale and moor, has terraces, a rock garden, cliff walk, ornamental pools — and a picnic area. A teashop is open at weekends. Plant sales area. The Gardens are open to the public, daily, from Easter to October 31 (10am until 6pm). Garden administrator (01756 720311 or 720269).

Linton-in-Craven: This relatively small village (just off the B6160) developed round a pleasant green with a beck and bridges. One side of the green is dominated by the classical form of Fountaine's Hospital (constructed on the instructions of Richard Fountaine in 1721). Fountaine was timber merchant for the architect Sir John Vanbrugh, who may have had a hand in the design of the almshouses.

The 15th century Linton Church, which also serves Grassington, Hebden and Threshfield, has an isolated position by the river. The church incorporates some Norman work. Until 1866 there were two vicars, the reason being the presence of two lords of the manor, each of whom had the right to appoint a clergyman.

A footbridge over the Wharfe, the fourth to stand hereabouts, was constructed by Army engineers in 1989. The river goes white with fury as it descends a rock staircase. On the other side of the bridge is Grassington.

Grassington: In the height of summer, or when a Dickensian Fair takes place in December, Grassington

Kilnsey   *G. Dodd*

seethes with people, for it is a popular shopping place. It is easy to escape from a crowd by following local footpaths. Traces of Bronze and Iron Age settlements have been found at Lea Green, to the north, but the village itself had an Anglian origin and was awarded a market charter in 1282.

Grassington Moor, exploited for lead under the Dukes of Devonshire, led to a local building boom. Many former miners' cottages have been converted into attractive homes for local people and the many off-comers who find Grassington a most desirable place to live.

One of the car parks is adjacent to Colvend, a Yorkshire Dales National Park Centre (01756 752774). There is usually stiff competition for parking places in the cobbled Square.

Upper Wharfedale Folk Museum, in two former miners' cottages, features lead-mining, minerals, craft tools, Dales farming and railway memorabilia. Open daily from April 1 to September 30 (from 2pm to 4-30pm) and from October 1 to March 31, Sat-Sunday, 2pm to 4-30pm. Admission 40p, with special family and children's rates (01756 752800).

Events: A summer festival with "big names" and music ranging from jazz to classical, also featuring lectures and poetry readings (01756 752096). An art exhibition in the Town Hall is another summer attraction.

Greenhow Hill: With a stimulating blend of motoring and mountaineering, a visitor reaches the airy heights of Greenhow Hill. This mineralised tongue of land, reaching 1,200ft between Grassington and Pateley Bridge, has been the setting for frantic lead-mining. The local pub is called The Miner's Arms.

Miners of the mid-19th century were sinking a shaft near the Stubbe or Stump Cross when, at about 50ft, they entered a cave system, which had been sealed off in the last Ice Age. The system, known as Stump Cross Caverns, is now a major tourist attraction, to be explored walking on firm paths and with imaginative electric lighting to show off the appeal of

Kettlewell   *Stanley Bond*

calcite formations.

Fossil bones aged between 30,000 and 200,000 years (and including bison, reindeer and wolf) have been recovered. Open daily from Easter to October; at weekends in November and December. In winter, by appointment. Parties: (01756 752780). Or (01423 711042).

Conistone and Kilnsey: Conistone was established 12 centuries ago but most buildings are 17th century and barns and the village school have been converted into residences in recent times.

Conistone church (somewhat isolated from the village) is one of the oldest in the dale. A comparatively new church, at Scargill, a Christian conference and holiday centre a short distance up the dale, has a high-pitched roof, in the style of a Scandinavian longhouse.

At the top side of Conistone, a narrow limestone ravine leads to the Dib. The slurring of stones under boots creates an eerie sound in the confined space.

Conistone affords a view (though not the best) of Kilnsey Crag, against which the Wharfedale glacier rubbed shoulders. A substantial river bridge links the two villages.

Kilnsey, which evolved from a grange of Fountains Abbey, and has not grown much since (while acquiring a massive limestone quarry), is the best viewpoint for the Crag's ponderous bulk and massive overhang. Village and Crag are now reflected in water at the Kilnsey Park Trout Farm, which is fed by spring water and yields pampered trout. In conjunction with fish-farming is a Dales Life Centre, plant nursery and the ubiquitous coffee shop. (01756 752150).

Kettlewell: An arc of parked cars near the river bridge testifies to Kettlewell's popularity. This village was divided between monastic establishments-Coverham, Fountains and Bolton. The village thrived with textiles and lead-mining. The church, of old foundation, was restored by the Victorians.

Kettlewell has long been a "watering hole" for travellers and there are three good pubs. Motorists with the spirit of adventure head for Park Rash, intent on driving up the fearsome zig-zags and crossing the tops to Coverdale. Walkers are "spoilt for choice", one recommended route involving a circuit, to and from Arncliffe in Littondale. For more gentle exercise, the riverside walk to Starbotton is recommended.

Buckden: In the days of Langstrothdale Chase, here lived some of the foresters employed by the Percies and, later, the Cliffords. (The Misses Stansfield, of Buckden House, kept fallow deer in the area within living memory).

The road pattern is a letter Y, with the left prong heading for Hubberholme and the source of the Wharfe. The right prong makes for Cray, Kidstones Pass and Bishopdale. A considerable acreage is now owned by the National Trust, who are renovating some of the old property, including walls and field barns.

Hubberholme: A forest chapel evolved into the church for a large but thinly populated parish.

Hubberholme's squat, battlemented tower peeps above a collection of yew trees. The churchyard (in which the ashes of writer J B Priestley were placed) extends to the edge of the infant Wharfe.

Within the church, look out for mice (wooden mice, on the pews, testifying these came from the workshop of Thompson of Kilburn). The rood screen is a rarity. A stained glass window commemorates the Falshaw family, resident in the dale for 1,000 years.

The George Inn (across the river) once belonged to the benefice. It is the setting, in January, for the Letting of the Poor Pasture (land left to provide an income for the impoverished members of the community).

Langstrothdale is a good picnicking area (with paddling possibilities near Yockenthwaite for children and those who are young at heart). At Beckermonds, where two lively becks meet, the Wharfe is born. The road from Beckermonds crosses Fleet Moss which, at 1,934ft, is the highest road in the county of North Yorkshire.

Littondale: This classic U-shaped dale (betokening glacial activity) is named after one of four settlements.

Dale Head Farm, Penyghent

An old name for the valley was Amerdale. Wordsworth referred to "the deep fork of Amerdale". The river Skirfare, often dry for much of its course, the water flowing underground, enters the Wharfe at Amerdale Dub.

Arncliffe, the largest village (and the only one on the south side of the valley) was developed on a delta of gravel, above the flood plain. A spacious green, with farms, cottages and the Falcon Hotel ranged around it, give the inhabitants the opportunity to keep an eye on each other. The church, dedicated to that grand old North Country saint, Oswald, is situated near the river bridge.

Bridge House, on the opposite side of the bridge from the church, is where Charles Kingsley, author of The Water-babies, had tea with Miss Hammond during an angling-walking holiday.

Littondale's road passes Litton and Halton Gill to peter out at Foxup. The road from Halton Gill runs "back o' Penyghent" to Stainforth in Ribblesdale. It is one of the great scenic runs in the Dales, given clear weather.

HARROGATE AND NIDDERDALE

War Memorial, Harrogate   *B. Wray*

Nidderdale has been a Cinderella valley in the sense that when the Yorkshire Dales National Park was inaugurated, the upper Nidd valley was left out. Upper Nidderdale is something of a stonescape, with a tucked-away, scattered community of farmers and cottagers living at what is simply called Stean. Two enormous dams, built by Bradford Waterworks, occupy another upland area and may be visited from a handy car park.

At Brimham Rocks, near Pateley Bridge — which has been referred to as Little Switzerland — wind-eroded gritstone blocks have taken on fantastic shapes. At Knaresborough, the Nidd flows down an enormous limestone gorge.

Harrogate: Population 69,100. When William Slingsby discovered a mineral spring in 1571, it was the beginning of Harrogate's evolution into a fashionable spa. Initially, it was considered that four pints of sulphur water a day cured most ailments.

The Stray — 200 acres of grassland protected by ancient law and open to visitors — gives breezy, hilltop Harrogate an attractive open character. Many of the buildings were built in Victorian times and retain their original cast-iron canopies. Prospect and Montpellier Gardens sustain the Harrogate theme of being a Floral Town. The Valley Gardens lead on to pinewoods containing rhododendrons and, further still, to Harlow Carr Botanical Gardens. (For motorists, Harlow Carr is in Crag Lane, off the B 6162 Otley road; no charge is made for parking). On the 68 landscaped acres of Harlow Carr, the Northern Horticultural Society grows plants suitable for northern climes. Open every day, from 9-30 am, last admission being at 6 pm (or dusk if earlier). A charge is made for adults, with a reduced charge for OAPs and no charge for accompanied children. (01423) 565418.

Notable Buildings: Modern architecture is seen at the Harrogate International Centre, where a 2,000 seat main auditorium is interlinked with seven exhibition halls. The Royal Pump Room (01423 503340) built in 1842 to enclose the old sulphur well — which was for many years the main watering hole — has been restored and converted into a museum of local history. (Ask for a sample of sulphur water).

Spa treatments were conducted on wealthy visitors by the Royal Baths Assembly Rooms, built rather more than a century ago. The Turkish Baths are still open to the public daily.

Events: Spring Flower Show (April) (01423 561049).

The Great Yorkshire Show, mid-July (01423 561536).

An International Festival (summer) and Competitive Music Festival (first three week-ends in March) are well supported. Repertory is presented in a Victorian setting, the Harrogate Theatre.

Sports: Harrogate Cricket Festival, Country Ground, July. (01423 561301). Multi-purpose Sports Centre. Dry ski slope. Four golf courses.

Shopping: Innumerable shops of all kinds. Harrogate is considered to be the antiques centre of northern England and in Sept-October the Northern Antiques Fair is held at the Royal Baths Assembly Rooms.

Tourist information: Royal Baths Assembly Rooms, Crescent Road (01423 525666).

Knaresborough: Population 14,095. Three miles from Harrogate, with an enviable setting beside a deep limestone gorge. Knaresborough market place contains the oldest chemist's shop in England (1720). Buy some of the special lavender water, made (of course) to a secret recipe.

The (sparse) remains of 14th century Knaresborough Castle are on the cliff above the Nidd gorge. The dungeon has survived! In the grounds is the Old Court House Museum, its special exhibition relating to local effects of the Civil War (01423 869274).

Of special tourist appeal is a visit to the restored St Robert's Cave and Mother Shipton's Cave and Petrifying Well. Born in 1488 she is said to have fore-

Fountains Abbey

told, among many other things, the Spanish Armada of 1588.

Events: Bed race in June.

Sports: Knaresborough Pool, opened in 1990, has four lanes and associated leisure area with flume and spa facilities. Putting and tennis in the grounds of Conyngham Hall. Putting and bowls in the Castle grounds.

Tourist information: 35 Market Place (01423 866886).

Fountains Abbey and Studley Royal: Four miles west of Ripon (off the B.6265), and nine miles north-west of Harrogate is Fountains Abbey. Presiding over an 800-acre estate it is the largest monastic ruin in Britain and was awarded World Heritage status in 1987.

The Abbey, founded by Cistercian monks in 1132, now has a stately setting in 18th century embellishments — the water gardens and ornamental temples of Studley Royal, now splendidly restored by The National Trust and worthy of being called, as it was two centuries ago, "The Wonder of the North".

A charge is made to visit Fountains. The Abbey and water gardens are next to the 400 acres of a deer park where red, fallow and sika deer are to be seen at close quarters. In the deer park, for which

The Druids' Idol at Brimham   *Bill Pates*

there is free access all the year, during daylight, is the ornately-decorated St Mary's Church.

At Fountains Abbey, guided tours, family activities and floodlit evenings provide a varied programme. The estate is open all year, daily except on December 24 and 25 and Fridays in Nov, Dec and Jan. Events: Floodlit Evenings. Restaurant. Shop. (01765 608888).

Ripley: Now (happily) by-passed, the village of Ripley has a French character, having been modelled as such for Sir Wm Amcotts Ingilby in 1827. The Hotel de Ville, or Town Hall, was added in 1854.

No less than 28 generations of Ingilbys have lived at Ripley Castle over a spell of 600 years. The Castle, often used for cinema and television films, has a walled garden and is set beside a deer park where there are lakes with waterfowl. Admission charge for guided tours during which items shown include Civil War armour to Venetian chandeliers.

Brimham Rocks: The area, which belongs to the National Trust, lies off the B 6265, some eight miles south-west of Ripon and 10 miles north-west of Harrogate (along the B 6165). Charge for parking.

Here there is 300m year old gritstone weathered into many fantastic shapes. Moorland setting. Self-guided trail leaflet. Information Centre, shop and refreshment (01423 780688).

Pateley Bridge: Population 2,100. A busy little town, consisting mainly of a steep main street where, in summer, there are so many flower arrangements — from hanging baskets to flower-filled stone troughs — the town (with Bewerley) has twice won the Britain in Bloom competition.

Pateley's old-time prosperity depended on lead-mining, quarrying and flax. All three are featured at the Nidderdale Museum, which won the National Heritage Museum of the Year award in 1990. Exhibits recall the hard lives of the folk of the dale in grand-mother's day. Open 2 pm to 5 pm. In summer, every day; from October to Easter, Sundays only. Free car park (01423 711225).

Events: Nidderdale Show, held in September at the very end of the Dales show season.

Sports: Nidderdale Recreation Centre, Low Wath Road (01423 711442).

Glasshouses: Just south of Pateley, the old flax mill is now devoted to country wines, a gallery and display of antiques. Traditional fruit wines are produced in the vaulted cellars. The wine-tasting room houses a water turbine. A former steam engine room is a tea-room, overlooking the River Nidd. (01423 711947 or 711223).

Tourist information at Pateley Bridge: 14 High Street (01423 711147).

Gowthwaite Reservoir: Between Wath (where a former mill has a gigantic outdoor wheel) and Ramsgill is a shallow reservoir built to compensate riparian owners for water taken out of the system at the big dalehead reservoirs.

The reservoir is outstanding for wildlife, especially birds. At Gowthwaite, rare birds are regulars.

Lofthouse and Reservoirs: Just beyond Lofthouse, on the right, is the start of the road leading to the reservoirs of Angram and Scar House. A small charge is made for visitors' cars and at the end of the road is a large car park, with toilets — in the wilderness! Footpaths permit the exploration of this High Pennine district.

How Stean Gorge: The limestone gorge, beside a road which begins just beyond Lofthouse (turn left) has a maximum depth of 70 feet. A visitor explores it on footpaths and bridges. Caves await exploration. Children's play area. Free car park for patrons. The gorge is open all the year, from sunrise to sunset. (01423 755668 or 755666).

Middlesmoor: The first/last village in the dale, depending on which way you approach it. For motorists, it's the last. After a steady climb from Lofthouse, the traveller enters constricted streets. There is a car park where the tarmac ends. The churchyard is a vantage point for Nidderdale, the clear-weather view taking in Gowthwaite reservoir.

THREE PEAKS AND NORTH RIBBLESDALE

This is classic limestone country. Carboniferous limestone, hundreds of feet thick, over-tops the ancient slates. Walk towards Ingleborough from the Hill Inn, Chapel-le-Dale, and you will encounter one of the scenic glories of Yorkshire — the limestone pavement and natural shafts galleries which are the potholes and caves.

Settle and Ingleton are well-tuned to tourism. Clapham is a favourite approach to the summit of Ingleborough. Horton-in-Ribblesdale is the usual starting point for the Three Peaks Walk, taking in the summits of Penyghent, Whernside and Ingleborough (twenty-five miles, with some 5,000 feet of climbing).

North Ribblesdale bears the enormous sores of quarrying, yet each quarry face provides an insight into local geology. Deserted quarries make prime nature reserves! Chapel-le-Dale (between Ingleborough and Whernside) abounds with natural wonders, including White Scar Cave, where passages are draped with calcite formations.

At Gaping Gill, on the eastern flank of

Horton-in-Ribblesdale

Ingleborough, a mountain beck leaps 340 ft into a chamber of cathedral size.

Settle: Old Settle snuggles against a limestone knoll, Castleberg, which may be ascended (with care) using an old zig-zag path. The little market town is sheltered from the north by Giggleswick Scars, alongside which runs Buckhaw Brow (now by-passed by the A.65) which is one of the best-known roads in the Dales.

Settle has held a market charter since 1249. On market day (Tuesday) stalls sprout like mushrooms in the market place, which is shadowed by the Shambles (formerly butchers' shops) and by a whimsical Town Hall, which someone described as being Jacobean Gothic.

Also in the Market Place is the "Naked Man", formerly an inn, now a cafe and cake shop. Notice from the effigy on the wall that this naked man had some buttons sewn on his chest. Ooch! A few minutes' walk from the Market Place is The Folly (1675), an architectural extravaganza.

Victoria Cave, on the scars behind the town, was one of the great "bone caves", with evidence recovered of animal life 120,000 years ago. The Museum of North Craven Life (which in the summer of 1994 was being re-styled) tells the story of Settle's evolution.

Shopping: Although the town's shops are somewhat less varied than they were, many visitors rejoice in the abnormally high number of antique shops. Two supermarkets, gift shops and several cafes meet local and tourist demands.

Transport: Settle has grown up in some isolation, which gives it a distinctive character. The bus service north of the town is sparse. Buses do run up the dale to Horton-in-Ribblesdale and down to Skipton. The town is on the famous Settle-Carlisle railway line.

Entertainment: Occasional special events at Victoria Hall. Settle has a rich musical life, with concerts at Settle High School, Giggleswick Church and other venues.

Sports: Rugby and football clubs. Indoor swimming pool (01729 823626).

Exhibitions and also tourist-orientated lectures (in summer, see local posters) at Watershed Mill, a former cotton mill just off the Langcliffe road. Also The Dalesmade Centre, rock and fossil shop, coffee shop, craft demonstrations. Open daily, except Christmas Day, from 10 a.m. (01729 825202).

Tourist information: Town Hall, Cheapside (01729 792809).

Langcliffe: A village with a green which stands between the Ribble and the limestone scars. A footpath between Langcliffe and Stainforth passes the Hoffman Kiln, at Craven Quarry, a German invention which was introduced to this district for the continuous burning of limestone, sidings providing ready access for the despatch of lime via the Settle-Carlisle railway.

A footpath from Locks Bridge, going west of the Ribble, leads picturesquely to Stainforth's celebrated single-span bridge which made the old stony-ford (origin of the name Stainforth) redundant when it was built in the 1670s. (The bridge was one of the first Yorkshire possessions of The National Trust, being handed over in the 1930s).

Goatscar Lane (initially steep) leads to Catrigg Force, a double waterfall (take care, especially in wet weather, when the limestone may be slippery). It was a waterfall visited by the composer Elgar, a friend of a Giggleswick doctor, C. W. Buck.

Helwith Bridge: Not a pretty place, but one full of interest for industrial archaeologists, for at five little quarries hereabouts Horton Flags were removed and shaped into flagstones, water cisterns, stone "benks" for dairies and even vats for brewing. An old quarry at Helwith Bridge, now full of water but fed by springs, is a fishery.

Horton-in-Ribblesdale: The village is mid-way (some five miles) between Settle and Ribblehead. Horton is dominated to the west by the face of Beecroft limestone quarry and to the east by Penyghent. St Oswald's Church (which, backed up by Penyghent, is the subject of a classic Dales photograph) is squat, with a battlemented tower, Norman doorway and nave arcades and also a west window featuring fragments of old stained glass, including the mitred head of Thomas á Becket.

Notice the considerable use of the blue-grey Horton Flags in the church yard, as flagstones, roofs

Settle   *E. Gower*

of lych gates and gravestones.

Penyghent Cafe, closed Tuesday, has a novel "booking out" system for Three Peaks walkers. Climb Penyghent, following the Pennine Way up a green lane beginning near the old vicarage.

Selside, the next settlement along the road to Ribblehead, is the place to park for a visit to Alum Pot, one of the major natural shafts of Craven. A stream pours into the hole. Keep well away from the edge. Alum Pot is on land where no public right of way exists. A notice at Selside indicates where a small payment to visit the pothole should be made.

Ribblehead: This tract of open ground is dominated by Whernside and the 24-arch Ribblehead Viaduct, on the Settle-Carlisle railway. Ribblehead can

Thornton Force, Ingleton

look Blackpoolish on a sunny day in summer. Walkers leave their cars here before tackling Whernside (2,414 ft) or crossing Blea Moor to Dentdale. When a "steam special" is due, the area fills up with railway photographers.

Chapel-le-Dale: The Hill Inn has a name relating to Ingleborough. Watch out for the sign (at the bottom of the slope on the Ingleton side of the Hill Inn) directing travellers to St Leonard's Church, once a distinct parish but now served by the Vicar of Ingleton.

Railway interest abounds. Inside is a memorial to those who died during the construction of the Settle-Carlisle. In the yard are a few marked graves. About 200 people — navvies and members of their families — lie in unmarked graves.

White Scar Cave a well-known show cave runs to Battlefield Cavern, with its tumbled boulders and assembly of delicate straw stalactites suspended from the roof. Open from 10 pm every day except Dec 25. (015242 41244).

Ingleton: The A65 by-passes the older part of the village. The parish church has an ancient tower and a body which has been periodically renewed. Ingleton was a former mining and quarrying community. It rose to prominence as a tourist village with the arrival of the railway in 1849; soon the glens of Twiss and Doe were opened out by the making of paths and bridges. The visitors were able to admire a variety of waterfalls, culminating in Thornton Force (46 ft). The water pours over an amphitheatre composed of limestone which rests on the old slaty rocks.

Market Day: Friday.

Sport: Heated open-air swimming pool (015242 41049). Annual Three Peaks Race.

Tourist information: (015242 41049).

Clapham: For many years a part of the Ingleborough Estate of the Farrer family, the village is very much the creation of this family. In the 19th century, they transformed a farmhouse into Ingleborough Hall; dammed the beck to form Ingleborough Lake, also providing the village with a waterfall as a head-piece, and planted extensive woodland.

Clapham impresses by its venerable, well-wooded appearance. A walk beginning near the church passes through tunnels which were created to extend the grounds of Ingleborough Hall before gaining an attractive green way between drystone walls.

Clapham has an National Park Centre (015242 51419) in the old Reading Room; there is a large adjacent car park. Several shops have been opened. A Cave Information and resource centre offers a film show and a glimpse of archaeological and historical material about Ingleborough Cave. The Centre is open daily from Mar 1 to Oct 31 and is open at week-ends and by arrangement during the winter months (015242 51242).

Most walkers head up through the Woods (small charge for admission) and the limestone valley beyond to visit Ingleborough Cave, which is open daily, with an attendant shop.

Gaping Gill, on the moor beyond Trow Gill (well-used footpath leads to it, but keep away from the edge of the hole) may be descended by bosun's chair and winch when potholing clubs hold meets here on Spring and Summer Bank Holiday weekends. The descent is free; a charge is made for the return!

6 INDUSTRIAL HEARTLAND

by Eileen Jones

They used to call it the Grand Tour. The idle rich, the debutantes, the convalescents and the curious wealthy would set off on a well established cultural route. The historic cities and the art treasures of Europe, and principally Italy, were their goal, and they travelled on trains like the Orient Express. London was only for Americans, and nobody came looking for culture in Yorkshire.

Now all that has changed. Today they call it the industrial heritage trail, and places like Leeds, Bradford and Sheffield are on the itinerary. And if they don't actually travel here by rail, then within a matter of days they are bound to have taken a ride on a steam train.

It took men and women of vision and imagination to harness what remained of Yorkshire's industrial

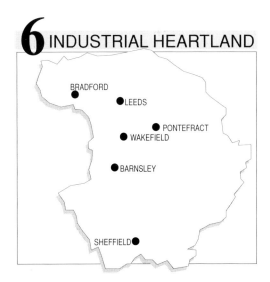

past and turn it into a modern tourist boom. The process developed apace with the decline of the traditional industries such as textiles and coal mining. And while the county's major towns and cities have generally survived economically by diversifying and experimenting, they have also thrived by promoting an image based on the best of the old and the new.

Who would have believed that leisure time in the late 20th century would be spent inspecting the working conditions and machinery of the industrial revolution? That holidaymakers would actually pay to be guided round an underground coal seam by a redundant miner? But the concept worked, and proved phenomenally successful. Wool textiles in Bradford, brewing in Leeds, steel making in Sheffield, coal mining in Wakefield are all part of an industrial heritage that fascinates tourists today.

The industrial heartland has art and culture as well, of course. There have long been visitors to the galleries and gardens of Harewood, the ruins of Kirkstall Abbey, and the eclectic displays at municipal muse-

Cartwright Hall, Bradford   *Camera Crew*

ums. To these, and to the industrial showpieces, have been added modern national museums — of photography and television, and of childhood.

Their fascination is matched by convenience: many of the attractions are in city centres, or on well served bus routes in the suburbs. They are easy to find and easy to reach, and they are usually weather proof. If you are spending a week's holiday in the Dales or the Peak District and there's a bad forecast, then you can fill a whole day in Leeds or Sheffield and nothing is spoiled by rain.

Culture vultures fill day after day, and come with no other purpose in mind. They know that the cities have good hotels, excellent restaurants and plenty to do in the evenings.

We have taken a look at the principal centres of Leeds, Bradford, Sheffield and Wakefield, aiming to include as many stately homes, museums and other attractions as possible, with some examples of what is available in outlying areas.

Leeds

Population 706,000. Leeds folk have never been lacking in self confidence or civic pride and there was something about the label 'England's second city' which inferred that there might be one place even better. It was also disputed by Birmingham and Manchester which had larger populations. So Leeds has opted for 'capital of the north', which irritates Mancunians but as they don't live in Yorkshire their opinion doesn't count. That, anyway, is the Yorkshire way of looking at life.

Leeds is brash and relatively affluent. It attracts new business and manages to retain some traditional industry. Its skyline, viewed from the essential though often jammed inner ring-road, is cluttered with new buildings, many of them in a classic red brick style which has won local architects both praise and abuse. It has a strong cultural tradition, a nationally acclaimed new playhouse, and the home of Opera

North. There's top class football, Test cricket and international swimming.

There's also The Waterfront, a transformed once-derelict area centred on the Leeds-Liverpool canal and the River Aire. Created from an ambitious partnership between the public and private sectors, The Waterfront now includes new hotels, a massive new brewery museum, office and commercial projects, the Granary Wharf and canal basin with its popular craft market, and industrial museums at each end of the renovated section. The Royal Armouries Museum, due to open in 1996, is also to be located here.

The city centre is dominated by modern development, which hides much of the remaining Georgian, Victorian and Edwardian building, although the Victorian Town Hall with its baroque clock tower and massive stone lions, stands proudly visible. Nearby, around a corner and almost hidden in a side street is St Anne's Cathedral, completed around the turn of the century. The centre still looks rather patchy and piecemeal, as the main shopping areas have been developed over the years and lack cohesion.

Shopping: The St John's and Merrion Centre precincts have found themselves rather stranded north of The Headrow. The busier and classier shops are found in and around the Bond Street and Schofields centres. Big department stores, all the high street names, independent specialists, the unusual and the quirky are all here. Ethnic and alternative specialities at the Granary Wharf craft shops, also the shops at Hyde Park corner a mile out of the centre on the fringe of student territory. Collectables at the recently restored Corn Exchange. The Victoria Quarter incorporates refurbished arcades and covered streets, with continental style pavement cafes and top quality shops. Huge Edwardian indoor Kirkgate market, Mon — Sat, early closing Weds. Open market Tues, Fri, Sat. Secondhand market Thurs.

Transport: The M1 and M62 cross just a few miles south of the city centre. M621 motorway takes traffic literally into the centre. Big rail interchange with good

Leeds Town Hall

local and national connections, including London in under two hours. National Express coach station on Wellington Street, central bus station for local services off Vicar Lane. Supertram scheme is under way. Leeds-Bradford Airport is at Yeadon, about 8 miles west of the city, domestic and international flights.

Entertainment: Cinemas — Cannon three screen cinema, Vicar Lane (01132 452665). Odeon, five-screen, The Headrow (01132 439821). Cottage Road Cinema, Headingley (01132 751606). Hyde Park Cinema, Brudenell Road, Headingley (01132 752145). Showcase, 10 screen out of town complex, Gelderd Road, Birstall (01924 420622).

Theatres — West Yorkshire Playhouse, Quarry Hill Mount — acclaimed new two-auditoria centre, gallery, bar, restaurant. Classic British and European drama, including world premieres. Resident rep company and visiting top theatre companies. Daytime happenings such as music workshops, circus performers, play readings (01132 442141).

Grand Theatre and Opera House, New Briggate —

Victorian traditional home base for Opera North, also mainstream drama and West End musicals, and ballet (01132 443509).

Civic Theatre, Cookridge Street — mixed programme venue with good amateur and professional drama, modern dance, recitals, concerts etc (01132 456343).

City Varieties, The Headrow — made famous by TV's The Good Old Days, this is England's oldest music theatre. Twice yearly music hall season, plus contemporary concerts, cabaret, light opera, pantomime etc (01132 425045).

Leeds Town Hall, The Headrow — venue for top classical music events, concerts, the Leeds International Concert Season, the triennial International Piano Competition etc (01132 476962/455505).

Yorkshire Dance Centre, St Peter's Square — home of the Phoenix Dance Company, the city's own professional contemporary touring troupe. Also dance classes for all ages (01132 426066).

Leeds Civic Hall

Lunchtime chamber music recitals, City Art Gallery (01132 478303).

Leeds has numerous venues for rock and pop concerts, folk music and jazz, and a lively nightclub scene. General jazz enquiries: 01132 742486. West Yorkshire folk scene: 01535 606939. Concerts advertised locally.

Sport: Leeds United FC, league soccer, Elland Road (01132 716037). Yorkshire County Cricket Club, Headingley (01132 787394). Leeds RLFC rugby league, Headingley (01132 786181). Bramley RLFC rugby league, Elland Road, Leeds (01132 711675). Horse Trials, Bramham Park (weekend following Spring bank holiday) (01937 844265). Swimming — Leeds International Pool, Westgate, hosts top events and is well used by locals. Also fitness gym (01132 443713). Golf — Leeds has 22 golf courses, including five municipal courses. Details from Tourist Information Centre. Ten-Pin Bowling — Leeds Bowl, Merrion Way (01132 451781). L A Bowl, Sweet Street, Holbeck (01132 421330). There are many sports and leisure centres in the Leeds area — full list from Tourist Information Centre.

Shows and fairs: Great St Valentine's Fun Fair, late spring. The beginning of a series of summer events of which the Lord Mayor's Parade (early June) is the most spectacular. Leeds Show, mid-August in Roundhay Park. Caribbean Carnival, late August — musical extravaganza with parades and street events. International Film Festival, October — up to three weeks of movie mania, with new films, premieres, previews etc at different venues. Leeds Lights, mid-November — switch on time for the Christmas city centre illuminations.

Galleries: City Art Gallery, The Headrow. Said to house the best collection of 20th century art outside London, but there's also a fine representation of 19th century painting as well. Also craft and design gallery with exhibitions and upmarket goods for sale. Next door, and linked via a covered bridge, is the Henry Moore Sculpture Centre. Mon-Fri 10-5.30 (10-9

Weds), Sat 10-4. Closed Sun, bank holiday Mons and
Tues. Free. (01132 478275).

University Gallery, Woodhouse Lane — permanent
collection of British 19th and 20th century paintings,
drawings and prints, plus temporary exhibitions.
Term time only, Mon-Fri 10-5. Free. (01132
332777). Cookridge Street Gallery. Part of the Jacob
Kramer College with work exhibited by local students
and outsiders, covering all forms of art, craft, design,
sculpture, photography etc. Term time only, Mon-Fri
9-5.30. Free. (01132 439931).

Museums: Leeds City Museum, The Headrow —
tradition museum with 'remember the empire' feel,
which makes a pleasant change from the municipal
museums which concentrate on local collections. Tues
-Fri 10-5.30, Sat 10-4. Free. (01132 478275).

Armley Mills. Close to Leeds-Liverpool canal two
miles west of city centre. Big industrial museum set in
what was once the world's largest woollen mill. But
the displays reflect the variety of the city's industrial
past, from textiles to engineering. There's a reconstructed 1920s picture palace with silent movies, and
— inevitably — some steam engines and static locomotives. Large free car park, gift shop, picnic area.
Tues-Sat 10-5, Sun 1-5. Adults £2, concessions £1.
(01132 637861).

Thwaite Mills. Another industrial museum, this
one lies between the River Aire and the Aire and
Calder Navigation, two miles south of the city centre.
This was a water powered mill, and the two huge mill
wheels are still turning; good video outlining the history of the place. Free parking, gift shop, cafe, lots of
displays. Tues-Sun 10-5, plus bank holiday Mons.
Adults £2, concessions £1. (01132 496453).

Abbey House Museum, Kirkstall Road (three miles
west of city centre). Domestic life recorded in
enchanting recreation of old streets in what was once
the gatehouse of Kirkstall Abbey (substantial
Cistercian ruin opposite worth looking at). You can
change decimal currency into old pennies to play the
slot machines. Highly recommended. Mon-Sat 10-5,

Sun 1-5. Adults £2, concessions (inc single parents, OAPs and unemployed) £1, children (5-15) 50p. (01132 755821).

Tetley's Brewery Wharf, The Waterfront — this is the thirst quenching industrial museum. It's a vast development in a riverside setting where a family could easily spend the best part of a day. There are recreations of pubs through the ages, brewery shire horses in action, a spectacular light and audio visual show, an organised tour if you want it, children's play area, and plenty of decent food and drink. You don't have to book in advance, but it is advised if you want to join the brewery tour at a time of your own choice (and you have to be over 18 to go on that, or with an adult if you're 14-17). Easily reached from M1 and M621, close to Leeds City station.

Daily 10-4 (last admission). Adults £4.50, concessions £3.60, children £2.50, also family ticket. (01132 420666).

Houses: Harewood House and Estate — a true aristocrat among tourist attractions and a very classy venue, not least because the family still lives at the magnificent 18th century house. The gardens and grounds are impeccably kept, the house boasts a wonderful collection of paintings and arguably the world's finest collection of Chippendale furniture, the view

Statue of Orpheus, Harewood House

from the terrace is spectacular and even the adventure playground is a class above the rest.

The terrace garden has been recently restored to its original layout, including elaborate Parterre hedging. Also the venue for musical and other events, including open air concerts, fashion shows, an annual steam rally and a country fair, and the estate has its own box office for bookings. (01132 886040). Harewood is seven miles north of Leeds on the A61 Harrogate road.

There is a bus service to Harewood village every 30 minutes from central Leeds and from Harrogate. Grounds and bird garden open daily, March to October, at 10. House, terrace gallery and church open at 11. Last admission 4.30, grounds close at 7. Freedom ticket (house, bird garden, grounds, gallery): £5.75 adult, £5 OAP, £3 child/student, £16 family. Bird garden and grounds: £4.50 adult, £2.50 OAP, £2.50 child/student, £12 family. Terrace gallery and grounds: £3 adult, £1 OAP and child. Season ticket: Family £25, couple £20, individual £15. (01132 886331).

Temple Newsam House, three miles from city centre off the Selby Road. Tudor-Jacobean mansion set in 1200 acres of parkland which is famed for its roses, rhododendrons, and a restored walled garden. Here too is the Home Farm with its centre for rare breeds of cattle, sheep, goats, pigs, hens etc. It is designed like an old style farmyard and you can wander among the animals. Children love it, although information is sketchy.

The house has a wonderful collection of decorative art all placed in original room settings, lots of fine silverware and Chippendale furniture. House open Tues -Sun and bank holiday Mons, 10.30-5.30, or dusk in winter. Adults £2, concessions £1, children (5-15) 50p. (01132 647321). Farm and gardens daily 10-4, earlier in winter. Free. (01132 645535).

Lotherton Hall, near Aberford (13 miles east of Leeds). Quite a homely atmosphere at this Edwardian country house, in spite of the opulent antiques and

Kirkstall Museum, Leeds

paintings on display. Oriental gallery with lovely Chinese ceramics. Surrounded by large estate which includes a well tended bird garden, where more than 200 species from around the world are kept, some rare ones being encouraged to breed in captivity. Open Tues-Sun 10.30-5.30 (closed 12-1), also bank holiday Mons, earlier closing in winter. Adults £2, OAPs £1, children 50p. (01132 813259). Bird garden open Tues-Fri 10-5, Sat, Sun and bank holiday Mons 11-6. Closed during severe weather in winter. Free. (01132 813723).

Parks and gardens: Roundhay Park, north Leeds. One of the biggest municipal parks in the country, very well tended, pleasant gardens, wilder woodland areas. Lots of sports fields, tennis courts, garden for the blind, bowling green, lake and lakeside cafe. Natural amphitheatre is used for galas, festivals and open air pop concerts. Large car park on Princes Avenue. Open daily dawn-dusk. Free. (01132 661850).

Canal gardens, Princes Avenue. A real treat for the garden enthusiast and the general visitor, this sheltered sun trap is home to the national collections of several plant species, and the North of England

National Rose Society trial grounds. Also Tropical World, a huge and unusual conservatory with waterfalls, butterflies, insects, fish in coral reefs, bats and orchids. This is one of the best free attractions in the whole of Yorkshire. Open daily 10-dusk, closed Christmas Day. Free. (01132 661850). There are many large and small parks and gardens open to the public in the Leeds area, details from Tourist Information Centre.

Nearby: The Middleton Railway, Hunslet. Steam trains every Sunday, April-Dec, also diesel service Sats April-Sept. Plus Santa specials, but otherwise few frills and gimmicks. This is a serious operation for devout steam enthusiasts. Fares and timetable: 01132 710320.

Tourist Information Centre, Wellington Street, Leeds. (01132 478301).

Bradford

Population 457,340. Once the world wool capital, modern Bradford is a city celebrating both its past and its present. The legacy of Victorian industrialisation remains, but it has become part of the multi-cultural, ethnically varied Bradford of today. It is not an ostentatious or wealthy city, for all the dominance of building society headquarters in the commercial centre. But it has a lively vitality, a good shopping centre which is relatively kind to pedestrians, some splendid Victorian architecture, and plenty of pigeons.

Bradford was one of the first places to capitalise on its industrial past and progressive present in an attempt to attract tourists. Cynics were gradually silenced, for there is a lot to see and do in and around Bradford, and coachloads of southern visitors really do make pilgrimages to the mill shops. The Museum of Photography, Film and Television gave the city national recognition, the Asian population gave it some of the best curry restaurants in the western world.

Shopping: Typical mix of high street chains and

smaller independents in the city centre, exciting and inexpensive shops along the arterial roads. Superb for exotic foods and spices. Early closing Weds. Daily Kirkgate indoor general market. Owlcotes out of town shopping centre between Bradford and Leeds at Pudsey, dominated by Marks and Spencer and Asda.

Transport: Bradford has its own link, the M606, to the M62 motorway, and a well signposted ring road system. Main line BR station, good local bus service.

Entertainment: Pictureville Cinema at National Museum of Photography, Film and Television. (01274 737277). Odeon, Princes Way. (01274 726716).

Bradford Playhouse and Film Theatre, Chapel Street — ambitious drama and movies. (01274 820666). Alhambra Theatre, Morley Street — glitzy, glossy venue for top level musicals, comedy, ballet,

United Reformed Church, Saltaire

drama. (01274 752000). Studio, Morley Street — the Alhambra's little brother, cosier, more experimental. (01274 752000). St George's Hall, Bridge Street — concert hall, (01274 752000).

Bradford Cathedral, Stott Hill. A lively cultural as well as religious venue. Excellent use of a fine building. (01274 728955).

Sport: Bradford City FC, league soccer, Valley Parade. (01274 306062). Bradford Northern RLFC rugby league, Odsal stadium. (01274 733899). Speedway, Odsal stadium. (01274 729443). Yorkshire Academy of Cricket, Park Avenue — county matches. (01274 391564). Richard Dunn Sports Centre, Rooley Avenue — multi-functional sports and leisure halls, splash pool etc. (01274 307822). Kart racing, Spring Mill Street. (01274 309455). Ice Skating, Bradford Rink, Little Horton Lane. (01274 729091).

Shows and fairs: Bradford Festival, mammoth three week bonanza of music, street theatre, drama etc at venues all over the city. Highlights include Lord Mayor's Parade, firework displays, and the Mela, a two-day spectacular of music and entertainment from all over the world, staged in Bowling Park. Mid-June. (01274 309199).

Museums: National Museum of Photography, Film and Television, Pictureville (city centre). Six floors of entertainment and information for all ages. Well designed, plenty of buttons to press, and a formidable array of old cameras. History of the media displays looking rather dated now, which reflects the speed at which changes have occurred. Entertainment includes the IMAX, Britain's largest cinema screen with its state of the art projection technology and film spectaculars and a cinerama cinema. Tourist Information Centre. Tues-Sun, 10.30-6, plus bank holidays. Entry to museum is free, but you pay to see the IMAX and Cinerama films. (01274 727488).

Colour Museum, Grattan Road — Unusual and worthwhile. Lots of inter-active displays. Tues-Fri 2-5, Sat 10-4, extended hours during mid-summer. Adults £1.10, concessions 65p. (01274 390955).

Bolling Hall, Bradford   *Camera Crew*

Bradford Industrial Museum and Horses at Work, Moorside Road. Converted mill site for this tribute to the efforts of the of the textile industry. Probably close to heaven for steam and other engine fanatics, but it doesn't bring the past to life (as the Calderdale Industrial Museum manages to do). On Wednesdays and some Saturdays they literally let off steam and operate some of the engines. The transport gallery is of more general interest, with the only surviving Bradford tramcar and trolleybus. Also a very good collection of locally manufactured cars, motorbikes and bicycles. Also home of half a dozen shire horses, including Norman, a 19 hands high grey, who is actually too big for most kinds of work. Resident stable master, complete with Victorian whiskers and bowler hat. Passenger rides in a horse drawn tram. Industrial history and entertainment combined and will definitely be the highlight for most visitors. Large free car park on site. The museum is well signposted, three miles from city centre on the A658 Harrogate Road. Tues-Sun 10-5, and bank holiday Mondays. Free, although there are donation boxes at strategic points inside the display areas. Small charge for the tram ride. (01274 631756).

Cartwright Hall, Lister Park. Grand building set in

parkland about a mile from the city centre. Marble floors and stone columns are the setting for galleries of real art treasures. Very lively for all its formal facade. Tues-Sun 10-6 April-Oct, 10-5 Oct-April. Closed Mondays except bank holidays. Free. (01274 493313).

Bolling Hall, Bowling Hall Road. More homely than Cartwright, but top quality exhibits, especially north country furniture, and a wonderful window of stained glass coats of arms. One mile from city centre off the A650 Wakefield Road. Tues-Sun 10-5 (10-6 after April 1), closed Mondays except bank holidays. Free. (01274 723057).

Undercliffe Cemetery, Undercliffe Lane — spectacular hillside site of 26 acres overlooking the city and graced with spectacular Victorian stonework. Recently restored by Bradford Council and now looked after by a voluntary group who are continuing the restoration work. (01274 642276).

Nearby: The towns of Shipley, Bingley and Baildon are not generally considered as tourist areas, but there are plenty of attractions packed within a few miles here. Best viewing is at the five rise and three rise 'staircase' locks on the Leeds and Liverpool canal at

National Museum of Photography, Film and Television

Bingley, a busy and attractive waterway used by all sorts of holiday craft. The locks can be reached from the centre of Bingley. Or you can park in Canal Road, about a mile from the town centre in a north westerly direction, opposite the moorings of the Airedale Boat Club. From here it is an easy few minutes' walk to the locks. A waterbus service operates between Shipley, Saltaire and Bingley. This is a traditional canal boat which calls at five bus stops along the route. For an up to date timetable contact Apollo Canal Cruises on 01274 595914).

The industrial hamlet of Saltaire is a bizarre and other worldly sort of place only a few hundred yards from the main A657 at Shipley. The whole settlement, which is now a conservation area, was built in the mid 19th century by Sir Titus Salt as a model village for the workers at his alpaca mill. The houses are dwarfed by the monumental proportions of Salts Mill, which is now the home of a David Hockney exhibition in the 1853 gallery. This occupies an entire floor of the mill, it's light and spacious and very classy.

Shipley Glen Tramway — delightful curiosity, positioned at the end of a residential estate (and in summer rather confusingly screened by trees — you won't see it until you get out of the car). Built in 1895, the cable hauled trams carry passengers for about a quarter of a mile through pretty bluebell woods, on narrow gauge track. Near the terminus is a small funfair, open at weekends and bank holidays, and during the school holidays (which does not mean everyone's school holidays, with Yorkshire's varied arrangements). A word of warning: this is not a highly developed tourist area, and signposting is limited. Use a good map, take the Baildon road out of Shipley, the second left at a small roundabout, and then watch for signs. Easter to Oct, Sat 1-5, Sun 10-6, also bank holidays, and Wednesdays during June and July. Santa Specials in December, parties welcome. Children — and pushchairs — can be accommodated safely. Fares: 15p down the line, 20p up, and 30p for the round trip. Children under three travel free. (01274

589010).

Bracken Hall Countryside Centre, about a mile from Shipley Glen. Small but busy visitor centre, surrounded by wildlife gardens. Free parking. Weds-Sun 11-5, April-Oct, also bank holidays. Weds-Sun 11-5, April-Oct, also bank holidays. Weds and Suns only Nov-March. Free. (01274 584140).

Tourist Information Centre, National Museum of Photography. (01274 753678).

Sheffield

Population 525,000. Sheffield has been in the doldrums for a few years. The city centre has been full of holes, with the accompanying noise of digging. The holes were needed for the installation of new power cables and to build the lines for the city's new Supertram. That's the bad news: the good news is that there's an end in sight, the holes will all be filled in, and Sheffield will have three major tram routes which should ease congestion in the city centre.

And there is Meadowhall — out of town shopping on a scale undreamed of, but it seems to offer what the people of Sheffield want: traffic free, weather free, masses of free car parking, its own bus and rail stations, and nearly 300 individual shops, from Marks and Spencer to French Dressing.

The shoppers deserted car-crazy streets and limited car parks. City centre workers still had lunch breaks to kill, but almost everyone else went to Meadowhall. Shops closed down, and stayed empty. To add to the air of dereliction, the building workers moved in to dig their holes in pavements and roads. The irony of Supertram, whose purpose was to persuade people to leave their cars behind, is that the first line to open was the link to Meadowhall.

So the people of Sheffield are understandably perplexed and sometimes angry at daily disruption. They are also, generally, immensely friendly people. The bits of their city untouched by hole-digging manage to look stylish and elegant. There are some delightful

Botanical Gardens, Sheffield   *Clifford Robinson*

architectural touches, including a splendid Victorian town hall, and culturally Sheffield has much to be proud of. And they are winning the battle against the car, with a well developed public transport system. For instance, if you want to visit the city centre, then it may well be best to leave your car at Meadowhall station (free parking) and catch the Supertram (service about every eight minutes). The city centre transport interchange is near the tram halt, information is easy to find, and buses are regular along routes to tourist attractions in outlying areas. There's a lot for the visitor to see and do, and if the big retail giants are pulling out of the city centre there are still smaller, individual shops, cafes and restaurants.

Shopping: Rather trendy designer shops in The Forum and Orchard Square. Crafts and interesting food well catered for. There are the indoor Sheaf and Castle markets, open every day except Thurs and Sun, and outdoor markets on Tues, Fri and Sat. There are suburban shopping centres at Hillsborough and Crystal Peaks, and then there's Meadowhall. For the statistically minded, there's 1.2 million square feet of shopping space, 282 retail outlets, 12,000 car parking spaces, 120 buses an hour and 250 trains a day, and something like half a million visitors every week. It's clean and spacious and well signposted, but it still feels claustrophobic, and disorientating for those without a good sense of direction.

Transport: Main line BR as well as buses and trams. Close to M1 motorway (Meadowhall is literally next to exit 34).

Entertainment: Multi screen cinemas at the Odeon (Arundel Gate, city centre. 01142 797602), at Crystal Peaks (01142 480064) and at Meadowhall (01142 569444).

Excellent theatres, notably the Crucible, Crucible studio, and Lyceum, all around Tudor Square and sharing the same box office number (01142 769922). Merlin Theatre — a Steiner community centre theatre set in woodland at Nether Edge (01142 551638). Montgomery Theatre, Tudor Square — local drama and non-mainstream films (01142 734102). University Drama studio, Shearwood Road — used by local groups, students, and foreign language performances (01142 826182).

Concert Halls: Sheffield Arena, Broughton Lane — arguably Britain's premier indoor pop concert venue (01142 565656). Sheffield City Hall, Barkers Pool — Philharmonic concert season plus rock, pop and comedy (01142 734550). The Leadmill, Leadmill Road — alternative comedy, Indie bands, flamenco dancing to name but a few (01142 754500). Octagon Centre,

Conisborough Castle, Doncaster   *Bilton*

Western Bank — part of the university, but open to public for pop and rock concerts (01142 753300).

Sport: League soccer — Sheffield United, Bramall Lane (01142 738955), Sheffield Wednesday, Hillsborough stadium (01142 343122). Athletics — Don Valley stadium, facilities for local athletes plus regular events up to international level (01142 560607). Ice Hockey — Sheffield Steelers, Broughton Lane (01142 561580). Greyhound racing — Sheffield Sports Stadium, Penistone Road (01142 343074). Speedway, Sheffield Sports stadium, every Thurs, April-Oct (01142 343074). Ponds Forge International Sports Centre, city centre. Vast and impressive new complex with Olympic size pool plus leisure pool with wave machine and two suspended 'flumes'. Large sports hall, host to world class events (01142 799766). Concord Sports Centre, Shiregreen Lane. Another large scale venue for squash, badminton, weight-training etc. (01142 570053). The Foundry, indoor climbing wall, Mowbray Street (01142 796331). Golf at Beauchief (01142 367274), Birley (01142 647262) and Tinsley (01142 560237). Hillsborough Leisure Centre — another pool with flume and water cannons, plus fitness suite (01142 312233). Graves Tennis Centre, Norton. Six indoor and 12 outdoor world class courts. Also indoor bowling (01142 839900). Sheffield Ice Sports Centre, Queens Road. Full size rink, skates for hire, cafe (01142 723037). Sheffield Ski Village, Parkwood Springs. Biggest artificial ski slope in Europe catering for novices and experts, nine different runs, lessons and equipment hire available (01142 769459).

Museums and galleries: City Museum and Mappin Art Gallery, Weston Park — sharing a home in a 19th century neo-classical mansion. The museum has a traditional series of displays — antiquities, local geology, wildlife — plus a section devoted to cutlery and Sheffield Plate. The art gallery is a little disappointing — no sign of the promised Pre-Raphaelites. Regularly changing exhibitions, education workshops, chamber concerts. Tues-Sat 10-5, Sun 11-5. Free (01142

726281).

Ruskin Gallery, Tudor Square — small and classy gallery which is home to a collection of paintings, drawings, illustrated manuscripts precious minerals and other items which John Ruskin put together for the people of Sheffield. Changing exhibitions on different themes. Also a craft gallery. Mon-Sat 10-5, closed Sun. Free (01142 735299).

Graves Art Gallery, Central Library, Tudor Square. Another pleasing collection in this cultural corner of the city, British and European art from the 16th century to the present day. Plus temporary exhibitions, classes, lectures. Mon-Sat 10-5, closed Sun. Free (01142 735158).

Abbeydale Industrial Hamlet, Abbeydale Road South. Don't shrink from the prospect of yet another industrial museum. This is one of the finest in the north. There are four water wheels, huge water powered hammers which were used for forging scythe blades, the world's oldest crucible steel furnace, a grinding hull and small hand forges, to name but a few. Go along and see things happening. Tues-Sat 10-5, Sun 11-5, plus bank holiday Mons. Cafe April-Oct. Adults £2.50, children and OAPs £1.25, disabled and UB40 free. Family ticket available (01142 367731).

The Shepherd Wheel, Whiteley Woods. Another water powered factory site on the River Porter, dating back possibly 400 years. Lovely woodland setting, but there's the strong impression of just how dreadful conditions were for the grinders who were working there until to the 1920s. Weds-Sat 10 -12.30 and 1.30-4.30. Sun 11-12.30 and 1.30-4.30. Closed Mon and Tues except bank holidays. Free (01142 367731).

Kelham Island Industrial Museum, Alma Street. Further evidence of Sheffield's historical prowess in steelmaking, with craftsmen demonstrating old machinery as well as a good exhibition of Made in Sheffield products. Mon-Thurs 10-4, Sun 11-4.45, closed Fri and Sat. Adults £2.50, children and OAPs £1.25, disabled and UB40 free (01142 722106).

Bishop's House Museum, Meersbrook Park. Pre-industrial history for a change, at this oldest surviving timber framed house in the area, built around 1500. Traditional style museum, with rooms done out in the fashion of different periods. Weds-Sat, 10-4.30, Sun 11-4.30, closed Mon and Tues. Adults £1, concessions 50p, family ticket available. (01142 557701).

Turner Museum of Glass, Dept of Engineering Materials, Sheffield University. Permanent display of hundreds of pieces of glassware. Mon-Fri, 10-4. Free (01142 768555 ext 5491).

South Yorkshire Fire Museum, West Bar. Who knows why little boys (and not so little ones) are so attracted by fire engines and hosepipes, but here's the place to keep them happy. Suns only, 11-5. Adults £1.20, concessions 60p (01142 752147).

Others: Heeley City Farm. Loved by children and school parties, a chance for city-dwellers to understand the reality of farm life. One of the best examples of its kind. Remember it can be mucky and smelly on the farm, so come prepared. Rare breeds, garden centre, children's play area, nursery garden. Daily 9-5. Cafe Weds-Sun 11-5. Free (01142 580482).

South Yorkshire Railway, Meadowbank. Worthy volunteers with ambitious plans to re-open stretches of track, owners of 25 engines, carriages, wagons and a signal box. The stuff of dreams for men and boys. Sat and Sun, 10.30-5.30. Adults £2, reductions for children (01142 424405).

Nearby: Cannon Hall Museum, Cawthorne, Barnsley. Georgian house set in 70 acre park five miles west of Barnsley. Period rooms with acclaimed collection of furniture, paintings including work by Constable. Exhibition of glassware, also museum of the 13th/18th Royal Hussars. Tues-Sat 10.30-5, Sun 12-5. Free. Also Open Farm behind the house, guided tours, spring lambs, donkeys and ponies, small animals corner, adventure playground and picnic area. Tues-Sat 11-4.30, Sun and bank hols 11-5. Adults £1.50, concessions £1 (01226 790270).

Elsecar Workshops, Barnsley. Early example of

multi-functional industrial estate used by blacksmiths, joiners, engineers etc, now a developing industrial and general museum and visitor centre. There's also a small steam railway which runs alongside the Dearne and Dove canal. Altogether a novel and rather different sort of museum, and well worth looking at. Daily 8.30-5.30. Different admission charges for various attractions, some free. General admission free (01226 740203). Tourist Information Centre: Peace Gardens (01142 734671).

Wakefield

Population 310,000. There are two startling points about Wakefield which strike the first time visitor. One is the cathedral, a glorious monument to the city's history since the middle ages, and bearing the tallest church spire in Yorkshire at 247 feet. The other is the quality of the tourist information. Glossy brochures and leaflets, booklets with all the relevant information in the right places, and an innovative self-folding street map.

Wakefield does impress. Not all of it, by any means, but the good bits are a credit to civic pride, industrial revival and opportunism. The old town was built on a hill above the River Calder and developed as an inland grain and cloth port, and Wakefield has retained its trading tradition. Today the cathedral is surrounded by pedestrianised shopping areas, leading to the markets and the modern Ridings Shopping Centre.

Shopping: As well as the inner city pedestrian precincts, the Ridings has most of the big name chain stores, a smaller version of Meadowhall.The Ridings can get very crowded and noisy, and the central feature glass lift linking the shopping malls with the car park is too small. But people who like shopping centres love this one. The markets are among the best in the north. Two market halls (early closing Weds) are linked by an open market (closed all day Weds).

Transport: South of Leeds, only minutes from the

Yorkshire Mining Museum

M1 and not much further from the M62. Mainline station on the intercity route between London and Leeds. West Riding bus and coach station caters for local, regional and National Express services.

Entertainment: Lots of pubs and clubs catering mainly for young people.

Cinema — Cannon, Kirkgate. (01924 373400). Theatre Royal and Opera House, Drury Lane. Small but lively cultural centre (01924 366556).

Sport: Three rugby league teams are based in the Wakefield district. Wakefield Trinity, Doncaster Road (01924 372445). Castleford, Wheldon Road, Castleford (01977 552674). Featherstone Rovers, Post Office Road, Featherstone (01977 702386). Racing: Pontefract Race Course (near junction 32 of M62). Flat racing from April — Oct, about 15 meetings in all, afternoons and evenings. Tote and off course betting. Children's playground and creche (01977 703224).

Lightwaves Leisure Centre, Lower York Street, Marsh Way. All the usual facilities including squash

Henry Moore sculpture at Bretton Country Park

courts and swimming pool with flume slide (01924 365005). Superbowl 2000 and Laserquest, Doncaster Road. Some 28 lanes of computerised ten-pin bowling, plus the hi-tech adventure game involving ray guns and universally sneered at by all those who have never played it (01924 382222).

Pugneys Country Park, Asdale Road. Lots of watersports in a newly created leisure complex on a former open cast mine site. Tuition, equipment hire, launching jetties. Charges for individual activities. Two miles from city centre off the Denby Dale road (01924 386782).

Golf — 18 hole course at Wakefield. Also 9 hole courses at Pontefract and Whitwood. (01924 360282). Athletics — Thornes Park stadium (01924 376900).

Shows and fairs: Festival of sport, early July, events

at various locations (01977 615198). Country Fair, Nostell Priory, late July (01924 863892). Wakefield and District Annual Show, Thornes Park stadium, late July. Mayor's procession, flower arranging, drama, dance, choral and other musical events, a whole programme of children's activities. Held over two days (01924 295787).

Galleries: Wakefield Art Gallery, Wentworth Terrace. Good representative art collection from 17th century Dutch to late 20th century paintings. Sculptures and drawings by Barbara Hepworth and Henry Moore. Not suitable for disabled. Mon-Sat 10.30-5, Sun 2.30-5. Free (01924 375402/295796). Elizabethan Exhibition Gallery, Brook Street. Former Elizabethan grammar school converted into stylish gallery. Closed between exhibitions so ring for details of events. Mon-Sat 10.30-5, Sun 2.30-5. Free (01924 295797).

Museums: Wakefield Museum, Wood Street. Traditional museum with a good section on local history. Mon-Sat 10.30-5, Sun 2.30-5. Free (01924 295351).

Yorkshire Mining Museum, Caphouse Colliery, Overton (midway between Wakefield and Huddersfield on the A642). Excellent museum, based at a former colliery. The former miners who conduct the underground tours (in a cleaned up, plenty of standing room tunnel) have a wealth of mining jokes. You wear a pit helmet and carry your own lamp and battery pack. It's pitch black down there, at a depth of 450 feet . On the surface there's plenty to occupy the claustrophobics, and the under fives who are not allowed down. There are pit ponies, the pit-head showers to inspect, and a rather nice 'nature trail' through woodland. Half way along is a good adventure playground. This was voted one of the best attractions by all members of the family. Large free car park. Daily 10-5 except Dec 24, 25, 26 and Jan 1. Adults £5.50. Concessions (students, OAPs) £4.50. Children under 16 £4. Under fives get in free. Family tickets and special rates for pre-booked groups. Entry fee includes the underground tour, and there is a part refund for surface-only visits (01924 848806).

Stephen G Beaumont Museum, Stanley Royd Hospital, Aberford Road. A real oddity housing displays about the history of the psychiatric hospital, with a padded cell. Open Weds only, by appointment (max 12 people per group). Free, but donations welcome and there's a booklet at £2 (01924 201688, ext 2170).

Houses: Nostell Priory, on A638 five miles from city centre. Dating from 1733 but built on the site of a medieval priory. Lovely mansion, home of Lord and Lady St Oswald, and owned by National Trust, with magnificent paintings, tapestries and furniture, including a Chippendale doll's house.. Occasional special events such as country fairs. April-Oct, Sat 12-5, Sun 11-5. July and Aug every day except Fri, 12-5, Sun 11-5. Bank holiday Mondays 11-5, bank holiday Tuesdays 12-5. Adults £3.50, children and concessions £1.80. Children under 17 free during school holidays (01924 863892).

Sandal Castle, Manygates Lane, Sandal (0ff A61 Wakefield/Barnsley road). Remains of medieval castle

Kirkthorpe, near Wakefield   *Stanley Bond*

on strategic site overlooking the city. Parliament ordered the demolition of the castle after the siege of 1645. Finds from excavations on view at Wakefield Museum. Daily, dawn — dusk. Free (01924 295351).

Nearby: Yorkshire Sculpture Park and Bretton Country Park, West Bretton. Are you ready to be confused? The sculpture park (YSP) is based at Bretton Park, the landscaped grounds of Bretton Hall, a college of Leeds University. It lies next to Bretton Country Park, which now houses the Henry Moore sculptures which used to live next door at the sculpture park.

The two are completely separate but the new arrangement is a joint project organised by the Henry Moore Foundation, YSP, and Wakefield Council. At Bretton Country Park there are now 16 Henry Moore monumental sculptures in a setting designed to explore the relationship between art and nature.

Next door, the YSP collection is made up of loans and a number of permanent works, with displays changing throughout the year. The country park has a small visitor centre, the YSP a wider range of facilities including pavilion gallery, shop and information centre, formal gardens, and a first rate cafe in a walled garden called the Bothy Garden. Both open daily, free. Bretton Country Park (01924 83055). Yorkshire Sculpture Park (01924 830302).

Hemsworth Waterpark and Playworld, Kinsley near Pontefract. A fun and fairly new attraction which claims to have 'inland beaches' beside the lake. Daily from 10, unless rain stops play. Free, but there's a £1 parking charge at weekends, bank holidays and during school holidays. £1 entry to children's adventure playground includes ride on model railway (01977 617617).

Newmillerdam Country Park. Designated area of outstanding beauty, with woods and lakeside walks, orienteering course, tea shop, craft shop. Special events organised by Wakefield Countryside Service include practical conservation days, treasure hunts, nature trails. Foresters often at work in the woodland.

Open daily. Free (01924 296203).

Anglers Country Park, Wintersett, between Crofton and Notton. Newly created park, with a big lake which is an important inland wintering wildfowl centre. Trout fishing in summer, visitor centre. Open daily. Free (01924 863262). Heath Village. Conservation area with houses dating from 17th-19th centuries, grouped around Heath Hall and Heath House. Village pub overlooking the common draws visitors from miles around. Pontefract Museum. Art nouveau building with eclectic displays, ranging from Roman relics to the production of liquorice, for which the town is famous (Pontefract cakes). Busy market town, remains of once strategic castle. Museum open daily Mon-Sat 10.30-5, Sun 2.30-5. Free (01977 797289). Pontefract Castle. Open daily. Free (01977 600208). Doncaster Leisure Park, The Dome. Said to be one of the country's largest multi-facility centres under one roof. Two level ice rink, six pool swimming hall with every conceivable gimmick, indoor village green, bowls hall, squash, gym, dance studio, cricket arena, massive fish and chip restaurant. To name but a few. Daily (01302 370888).

Tourist Information Centre, Town Hall, Wakefield (01924 295000/1).

7 THE SOUTH PENNINES AND BRONTE COUNTRY

by Eileen Jones

Aregion with an indistinct boundary, a dubious title and some peculiar claims to fame is, for many people, the very best corner of Yorkshire. South Pennines is really a misnomer, for the southern tip of the Pennine chain lies in Derbyshire. And a not insignificant stretch of this region labelled South Pennines actually lies over the boundary in Lancashire.

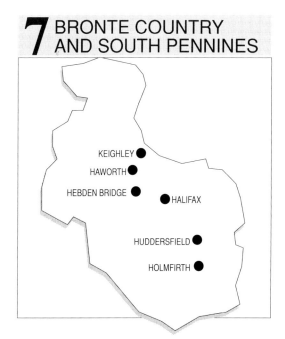

7 BRONTE COUNTRY AND SOUTH PENNINES

KEIGHLEY
HAWORTH
HEBDEN BRIDGE
HALIFAX
HUDDERSFIELD
HOLMFIRTH

So we have drawn our own rough boundaries of the Yorkshire South Pennines, starting from a line south of the Leeds and Liverpool canal, through the 'Bronte' country of Haworth and Keighley, to a focal centre point at Hebden Bridge, and then east and south via Halifax and Huddersfield to the moorland which fringes the Peak National Park.

At the northern end, recognition came through the inspired genius of three literary sisters; at the southern end it came via television through the spectacular popularity of three old men and a wrinkle-stockinged crone. 'Summer Wine Country' is now the accepted definition for the environs of Holmfirth.

In between lies a moorland landscape of unsurpassed grandeur and remarkable diversity. But though

Holmfirth   *Tim Stead*

wild in many places, it is not strictly a wilderness, for there is civilisation too close by for that. Any apparent wilderness is experienced only by the walkers who leave the marked paths and strike off across tussocks and peat. They might not see them — they certainly won't see them in the all too frequent mist — but the villages and towns are not really far away. And it is a cluttered landscape, criss-crossed by canals, dotted with old mills and restored mills, old farmhouses and restored barns, soaring railway arches, modern pylons and wind turbines. And everywhere the dry stone walls, thousands of tons of them.

It is a region where agriculture and industry have operated side by side and the relics of the past have become an intrinsic feature of the modern geography along with the unfolding valleys and the rocky out-crops. The industrial history links the settlements on the fringes of the moorland, where determination and enterprise once joined forces to eke out an existence with the villages and towns which grew on the strength of the textile boom.

The cottages clinging to the hillsides in Hebden Bridge, with their skylights so beloved by today's artistic community, were the homes of weaving out-workers employed by the big mills. And the mills themselves were built beside the streams and rivers tumbling from the moors where the power of water could be harnessed.

To appreciate the South Pennines you need to come here with a purpose. It simply will not do to arrive here on holiday, sit back and wait to be entertained: this isn't Scarborough. Nor is there the sense of peace and relaxation which is found in the Dales. This is a working region which, coincidentally, provides very well for tourists. Especially those prepared to become embroiled in day to day life, rather than the idlers and the moochers.

So come with a sense of direction and aim, be it lit-erary or artistic or energetic. Come and learn how to build a dry stone wall or take a course in orienteering. Hire a mountain bike or spend a literary retreat doing some creative writing. Make a tour of all the industrial museums for a very well defined history lesson, or set up home from home on a canal narrowboat. If you want to ride, the new Pennine Bridleway will soon be waymarked and signposted alongside the original Pennine Way which passes through this area.

Best of all, put on the walking boots. Because this relatively small area has crammed into it so much of topographical and natural interest, even the mountain bikers and the pony riders and the fell runners are travelling too fast to make intimate discoveries.

There are already-legendary circular walks like the 50-mile Calderdale Way and the 90-mile Kirklees Way, and there are linear waymarked trails like the nine mile Bronte Way, and the 12-mile Standedge Trail. But there are also unspoiled woods, streams and waterfalls, seldom used paths, heights and hollows, to be found off the beaten tracks. You can spend summer hours bilberrying beside an old pack horse bridge, or try to follow equally ancient causey stone routes through winter snow.

In winter the miles of peat-black moor can be iron hard on a morass so deep that only the foolhardy would venture there alone. In summer when the high land lies beneath the call of curlew and skylark, tired feet lift swirls of dust or sink into a black slurry. But these hills really are for walking.

From Holme Moss eastwards into the Holme Valley trees and rich green predominate, in contrast with the vast reaches of wind-bent grass and groughs heading west to Chew and south towards Longdendale. The area around Widdop, Gorple and Walshaw Dean where the Pennine Way drops down from Top Withins, is a lake district in miniature, though these are all man made reservoirs.

This is not the wettest part of England, whatever the natives may tell you. But it can often be misty, and this is not a swirling, tantalising mist (except in early summer after dawn) but a heavy, solid, damp blanket. You can trudge all the way up to Stoodley Pike and be rewarded with not even a glimpse of Lancashire.

Instead you can take to the woods where the mist draws in the horizon sharply and the eye is forced to notice the immediate — mosses and wild flowers and birds — rather than the skyline. Or you can pack up the boots for a better day and head indoors. In recent years, as the tourism potential of the South Pennines has been realised, a whole range of under cover attractions has been developed, by those who realised too that not everyone wants to battle with the elements.

There are few places in England so well serviced by local bus routes, while the train is a distinct advantage — especially at weekends — for visitors who want to get into the heart of the region. The valleys of the South Pennies were not designed with motorists in mind. It is quite feasible to organise train and bus links to some of the best walking country. The tourist information centres are extremely well equipped to handle transport queries. They also have details of guided walk programmes for those who prefer more sociable rambling.

The TIC is also the place to find recommended places to stay. Holidaymakers spending a week are far outnumbered by day visitors, but the provision of accommodation has improved dramatically in recent years. It also tends to be more individual and idiosyncratic than elsewhere, due partly to the number of converted farms, barns, and mills.

Haworth

Population 13,800. When the Brontes created their romantic heroes and heroines, did they imagine that 100 years later tourists would be tramping the moors looking for Wuthering Heights? That Heathcliff would be the name of a teashop, and Bronte a brand of biscuit?

It is impossible to tread the heaving cobbled main street, with its gift shops and olde herbalists and cafes, and ignore the influence of the Brontes. Equally, it is quite possible to forget that there is more to Haworth

Bronte Parsonage, Haworth   G. Bernard Wood

than this main street, and that the former village is now virtually a suburb of Bradford.

On a bank holiday the crowds are shoulder to shoulder, as they were on the terraces in the days before the all-seater football stadium, searching for Bronte tea towels and watching the jugglers outside the pub where poor brother Branwell would drown his sorrows. Better to come on a quiet day midweek, out of season, when some of the shops are closed, and then you can savour the atmosphere and get into the Parsonage museum without queuing.

Two features remain unspoiled. The books will outlive all the hyperbole. And the countryside around Haworth is magnificent, the heather moors with their drystone walls and old farmhouses, and the wind wuthering. The Americans and the Japanese are besotted by it all.

Shopping: Low on basic provisions, high on gingham capped jams and myriad chutneys. Frocks and jumpers, dried flowers and herbs, pots and paintings — none of it really remarkable and most of it available more cheaply elsewhere. Early closing Tues.

Transport: A couple of miles south of Keighley and very well signposted. Nearest main line station at Keighley, but steam train connections on the Worth Valley Railway. Local bus service links with Keighley, Bradford and Hebden Bridge.

Sport: Bowls and putting in Central Park. Pony trekking from various centres around the area.

Walking is by far the major recreational pursuit, and the Tourist Information Centre is well stocked with maps and guides.

Annual events: Bronte Society Annual Weekend, early June (01535 642323).

Museums: Bronte Parsonage Museum, to which the serious tourists make their pilgrimage. This is where the Rev Patrick Bronte made his home in 1820, and where his four surviving children spent most of their lives. The rooms, decor and furnishings are unexceptional and what you would expect, but there is something awe-inspiring about the manuscripts, the drawings, the personal letters and the miniature books. A later wing of the building houses exhibitions and a library with good research facilities (appointments only). Daily except for Christmas and a short break in January, 10-5 April-Sept, 11-4.30 Oct-March. Adults £3.60, children (5-16) £1.10, OAPs and students £2.60, UB40 £2.10. Also family ticket, and special rates for groups (01535 642323).

Haworth Parish Church. The Bronte family vault is here, also the Bronte Memorial Chapel. The church is actually a newer reconstruction incorporating part of the tower of the old church demolished in 1879.

Haworth Museum of Childhood. Small but pleasing collection of old toys, dolls, working model railways. Daily 10.30-5.30, Easter-Oct, weekends Nov-March. Adults £1, concessions 50p (01535 643593).

Nearby: Top Withins, ruined farmhouse high on the moors alongside the Pennine Way and three miles from the nearest road. Thought to be the inspiration for Wuthering Heights. Reached by way of Bronte Bridge and Bronte Waterfalls (not much to look at unless there's been heavy rain).

Penistone Hill Country Park. Not a park at all, but a bit of featureless raised moorland with car parks and picnic sites. One spectacular gorge which is the start and finish point for a number of local fell races.

The grave of Miss Lily Cove, in Haworth Cemetery. Absolutely no literary connections, but Britain's first woman balloonist and parachutist who died in these parts in 1906 when she became separated from her parachute during a demonstration performance.

Ponden Mill, Stanbury. Classier than most mill shops, this one calls itself a country store, and sells predominantly bedding and linen, but also gifts, crafts, books, clothes. Decent cafe. Open daily 9-5. Free parking (01535 43500).

Tourist Information Centre, West Lane (01535 642329).

Keighley

Population 45,120. Sadly dismal industrial town with some examples of domestic and commercial Victorian architecture which hint at a more gracious past. But it marks the boundary between industrial West Yorkshire and the rural Dales, and many a journey has to be made through the town to reach prettier destinations. There are a few good reasons for breaking the journey, and for those living or staying nearby, Keighley has some small but pleasant surprises. (Haworth, neither small nor surprising, has its own section.) Dining out is not one of them.

Shopping: The usual list of chain stores and high street names, on a small scale and visually uninviting. Market: Mon — Sat, early closing Weds.

Transport: On the A650 from Bradford. BR station, links with Leeds and the Settle-Carlisle line. Also steam railway (see below).

Entertainment: Keighley Playhouse, Devonshire Street (01535 604764).

Sport: Keighley Leisure Centre, Victoria Park. Trendy swimming pool with warm water, underwater lighting, water slide etc. Plus other sports, sauna, cafe (01535 681763). Horse Riding — Centres at Riddlesden, Flappit and Goose Eye (01535 642329).

Museums: Cliffe Castle, Spring Gardens Lane. Victorian wool baron's mansion with eclectic mix of displays. Outside there are gardens, aviaries, children's play area, cafe, large car park, small garden nursery. Seldom crowded, an ideal time filler for youngsters. Tues-Sun 10-5 (10-6 April-Sept) and bank holidays. Free (01535 618230).

East Riddlesden Hall. Very attractive Elizabethan manor house with walled gardens and duck pond, now owned by the NT. Tastefully decorated, with some good examples of old oak furniture, a collection of decorative pewter, and early kitchen utensils. Restored barn. Occasional family fun events, dancing and circus displays. Tearoom welcoming to families with small children, even if pushchairs can't be taken into the house. Easter-Oct, Sat, Sun, Mon, Tues, Wed and Good Fri. Also Thurs in July and Aug. 12-5, last admission 4.30. Grounds free. Hall: adults £3, children £1.50, family tickets available (01535 607075).

The Yorkshire Car Collection, Grange Street. Visual feast for motoring fanatics with comprehensive displays of veteran, vintage and classic cars. Gorgeously vulgar American classics too plus cars owned by the rich and famous. Daily April-Oct plus weekends throughout year except Dec, 10-5. Adults £3.50, concessions £2.50. Special rates for groups, car clubs. Cars available for hire (01535 690499).

Vintage Railway Carriage Museum, Ingrow. Collection of historic coaches based at one of the sta-

Keighley Car Collection   *Camera Crew*

tions of the Keighley and Worth Valley Railway (see below). Weekends, Easter and all bank holidays except Christmas Day, plus daily mid-June to end Aug, 11.30-5. Adults £1, concessions 60p, family ticket available (01535 646472 or 680425).

Keighley and Worth Valley Railway. This is the big daddy of all steam railways, Puffing Billy meets Thomas the Tank Engine. Small boys outnumbered considerably by grown men who give up their

The village church at Heptonstall, near Hebden Bridge. The archway is part of the ruins of the original church, built in 1260.

Clifford Robinson

weekends to chuff out of the sidings and back in again. A very well preserved line, owned and run entirely by volunteers, with vintage steam and diesel trains operating a regular timetable (more reliable than BR) from Keighley to Oxenhope via Ingrow, Damens, Oakworth and Haworth. Family events throughout the year, including hugely successful Santa Specials. All weekends and bank holidays through the year, plus daily mid-June-mid-Sept. Free small carriage museum at Oxenhope (01535 645214).

Tourist Information Centre, Keighley Town Hall (01535 618014).

Hebden Bridge

Population (including neighbouring Mytholmroyd) 12,651. It's known now as THE Pennine Centre, but in the 1960s Hebden Bridge was on its last legs. The mills were closing down, the young people were moving away and everything shut down for the weekend at noon on Saturday. But there were civic groups and individuals with vision. Today Hebden Bridge is famous. They have heard of the place in London, in Amsterdam and in Paris. Only no one is sure why.

It's not due to popular culture, as in Holmfirth. Sure, the television cameras have been around to film the Hovis advert, and to fill a few shots for a dated police series called Juliet Bravo, but there's nothing on the Summer Wine scale.

And there's certainly not an historical-literary tradition, although the periphery has claims: Poet Laureate Ted Hughes was born in Mytholmroyd, his estranged wife and writer Sylvia Plath is buried at Heptonstall, and Branwell Bronte is said to have manned the now-defunct railway station at Luddendenfoot. Today's resident population of the multi-storey terraced cottages clinging to the hillsides numbers an above average percentage of writers and poets. And sculptors and weavers. And, allegedly, vegetarians, sociologists and Guardian readers. There are definitely jugglers, for they run a circus workshop at their own juggling-ball factory up the hill at Old Town.

But none of them alone explains the magnetism of Hebden Bridge for tourists. Geography provides the rest of the answer, for here there is a spectacular and intimate relationship between town and topography, as a view upwards from Calder Holmes Park, or along the valley from any hilltop location, will confirm. Architects with an eye for shape and townscape wonder at the buildings which cling to the steep hillsides, while down in the narrow valley bottom road, river, railway and canal run side by side by side, leaving little other level territory.

Sundays are not much fun if you have to travel by car. Saturdays are remarkably less congested, yet Hebden is often more fun, with bands playing, Morris men dancing, or the local jugglers doing a bit of fire-eating practice on the marina. (It took a Dutch visitor to point out that a 'marina' strictly speaking has to be beside the sea; here they make do with the Rochdale canal and no one seems to mind.)

Hebden Bridge has not yet suffered the commercialised fate of Haworth, and there are still good general and specialist shops to be found although the gift shops, cafes and take-aways are increasing. There are some small commercial galleries, no major town centre museums and not a steam train in sight.

The restored Rochdale canal is a big attraction both on and off the water. The completion of work to unblock the canal at its Sowerby Bridge end, linking it with the Calder and Hebble finalises the navigation network from the Lancashire border, through Yorkshire and the Midlands to London. But beyond the towpaths, this is the centre of the green lungs of the industrial north, an imperfect paradise, perhaps, for walkers and horse riders and mountain bikers, but better than you'll find anywhere outside a national park. You can cycle on or off road, tackle the pack horse trails which form part of the infant Pennine Bridleway, while its rambling older brother the Pennine Way crosses through (near the sewage works, a mile to the west), and the 50 mile Calderdale Way has Hebden as a slightly off-centre axis. There is glorious walking country — for strollers or serious ramblers — in Hardcastle Crags, on the moors around Widdop, on the slopes of Stoodley Pike, in Cragg Vale and Jumble Hole Clough and Crimsworth Dean. And it's all lush and green because it rains a lot.

Shopping: Good for books, antiques, fashion, pottery, classy greetings cards, artists' materials. There are several mill shops, mostly selling outdoor clothing. No truly haute cuisine, but plenty of cafes and teashops. Second-hand market Weds, general market Thurs. Early closing Tues.

Transport: Between Halifax and Burnley on the A646. BR station links with Halifax, Leeds and Manchester. Parking is becoming a serious problem at weekends, particular on Sundays, and the trains do link up with (summer service) buses into the surrounding countryside.

Entertainment: Cinema, New Road (01422

Heptonstall   *Den Oldroyd*

842807).

Hebden Bridge Little Theatre, amateur and occasional professional drama (01422 843907).

Sport: Bowls, tennis, at Calder Holmes Park. Sports and leisure facilities at Mytholmroyd Community Centre (01422 883023). Angling on the Rochdale canal (licences from Tourist Information Centre). Fell running, around a dozen short, medium and long distance races start in or near the town (0161 485 1639).

Mountain biking — trails throughout the Upper Calder Valley. Access information plus local events from the Countryside Service (01422 886149 or 359454).

West Yorkshire Cycle Route: 150 mile circular road route linking railway stations around the Pennines and starting at Hebden Bridge. Map and leaflet from all Tourist Information Centres in the region.

Riding: South Pennine Packhorse Trails Trust produces maps and information on access etc. (01706 815598).

Shows and fairs: Swiss week, early June. Varied festivities celebrating links between the town and Ruetli, where the Swiss confederation was founded (01422 843903).

World Dock Pudding Championships, Mytholmroyd Community Centre. Mid-May. Competition for the best creation of this local delicacy made of dock leaves, oatmeal, onions and bacon fat, and taken very seriously locally and nationally (01422 883666).

Vintage Weekend. Mostly cars but other old forms of transport too, centred around Calder Holmes Park and the marina, usually first weekend in August (01422 843831).

Mytholmroyd Gala, last Saturday in August. An old-fashioned carnival with decorated floats, Sunday School queens, a pipe band, flower show, fell race etc. Best of its kind for miles around (01422 885193).

Pace egging. Ancient and symbolic plays celebrating the death of the old year and the birth of the new, performed in streets and squares throughout Calderdale on Good Friday and Easter Saturday, but most famously in Hebden Bridge.

Museums: Automobilia, Old Town. Transport museum with a good collection of early cars, vintage motorbikes and early bicycles. Base for vintage car rallies. April-Sept, Tues-Fri 10-5, Sat and Sun 12-5. Oct, Nov and Mar Sat and Sun 12-5. Dec, Jan, Feb Suns only 12-5. Open all bank holidays. Adults £2.20, concessions £1.50, family ticket £5.50. Under fives free (01422 842884).

Hebden Crypt, Museum of Myths, Legends and Horrors, Valley Road. Perfectly ghastly in concept and experience, but that's probably deliberate. April-Sept daily, 10-5, Oct-March Tues-Sun 10-5. Adults £2, concessions £1.50 (01422 845690).

Others: Hebble End. Converted canalside mill housing a few individual craft shops and workshops, plus the World of the Honey Bee exhibition. Daily in summer, limited opening in winter. Free to mill, Honey Bee £1.50 adults, 75p concessions (01422 845557).

Rochdale Canal. Calder Valley Cruising operate a regular service from the marina along a stretch of the restored waterway, going through one or more locks. Occasionally horse drawn boats (01422 844833).

Walkley Clogs. Traditional clog making is just a small corner now of this big mill conversion, now housing small shop units. This is one of the area's biggest tourist attractions, which says more about British shopping habits than about the merits of wooden-soled footwear. Claustrophobically crowded at weekends, when some individual units also charge an entry fee. Parking charge at weekends. Open daily (01422 842061).

The Circus Factory mill shop, Old Town. Home of Britain's top juggling equipment manufacturer — they also make unicycles — and you will usually find someone willing to demonstrate. Or eat a bit of fire. Talented visitors encouraged to show off. Open daily, May-Sept 11.30-4.30 (01422 843672).

Hardcastle Crags. A bitter disappointment for rock climbers, the actual 'crags' are small and easily unnoticed rocky outcrops. But they gave their name to the valleys of Hebden Dale and Crimsworth Dean, which converge at the hamlet of Midgehole, where there is a National Trust Car Park. Immensely popular, and the walk along Hebden Water to Blake Dean is glorious in any season. A mile from the main car park is Gibson Mill, a redundant cotton mill which has also seen life as a roller skating rink. There are buses to Midgehole Road, and along Widdop road in the summer. And you could even WALK from the railway station.

The Old Grammar School Museum, Heptonstall. Small and quirky museum combining old school furniture with displays of local history and crafts.

Heptonstall is a hilltop weaving village above Hebden Bridge, full of cobbles and courtyards and much more interesting architecturally than Haworth. It is virtually unspoiled by commercial concerns, which also means few parking spaces. There are buses from Hebden, or you could walk up the cobbled hill known as The Buttress (and up which local runners race with bales of hay on their backs for fun once a year). There are two historic churches, one dating from the 13th century and now in ruins, the other built to replace it in 1854, in the same churchyard. Here is Sylvia Plath's grave, and nearby Lumb Bank, once the home of Ted Hughes, is now the centre for the Arvon Foundation's creative writing courses. Museum open Easter — October, weekends and bank holidays, 1-5. Midweek visits by appointment. Adults 50p, concessions 25p (01422 843738).

Nearby: Stoodley Pike. Stone built phallic tower on the hilltop above Erringden, between Hebden Bridge and Todmorden. Erected to commemorate the defeat of Napoleon, it was struck by lightning and later rebuilt. Worthy objective for walkers, runners, mountain bikers and riders by any number of routes.

Dean Clough, Halifax

Inside the tower a dark, spiral staircase leads to a viewing platform for the best panorama of the whole Calder Valley. Small replica on the opposite side of the valley, the Pecket Memorial at Pecket Well, was built in memory of the dead of the First World War.

Todmorden. Mill town which once straddled the Lancashire border, now wholly in Yorkshire. Lacking the charm, the novelty-value and the hype of Hebden but not without its interesting features. Among them a neo-classical Town Hall, which is open to the public occasionally (check local TIC for dates) and the Todmorden Astronomy Centre, a truly unexpected planetarium on the road to Bacup, run by enthusiasts. Open for group bookings by appointment. (01706 816964). A group of steam enthusiasts have plans to establish a steam train centre based at the railway station. Also small and friendly craft centre in Lever Street (01706 818170) and various sports plus conservatory and aquarium in Centre Vale Park.

Tourist Information Centres, Bridge Gate, Hebden Bridge (01422 843831) and Burnley Road, Todmorden (01706 818181).

Halifax

Population 87,600. A surprisingly elegant and once prosperous Victorian mill town, Halifax has managed to survive the loss of its wool trade and emerge as the busy and functional capital of Calderdale. This is said to be the model which inspired William Blake's vision of 'dark Satanic mills', but Halifax has been sandblasted clean and thoughtfully restored.Imaginative pedestrianisation and a useful covered market housed under a magnificent Victorian roof.

The town hall, also extravagantly Victorian, was designed by Sir Charles Barry after his 'practice run' designing the Houses of Parliament. The parish church of St. John the Baptist is mid-15th century, with some parts dating from the 11th century. The Wainhouse Tower at King Cross is said to be the tallest folly in the country, built as a chimney for a dyeworks but used by the owner to spy into the grounds of a rival neighbour. It is open to the public on just a few days each year (01422 368725).

At Dean Clough a massive mill complex has been converted into a series of small units housing galleries, computer firms, even the national headquarters of a big food wholesaler. The Northern Ballet have their home in Halifax, so does the HQ of the world's biggest building society. It's unlikely that visitors would make Halifax their HQ for a week's holiday, but there's a good variety of wet-weather occupations for those staying elsewhere in the South Pennines.

Shopping: The shops and restaurants are not particularly sophisticated, but the quaint and the curious can be found gathered around the courtyard of the Piece Hall. Early closing day officially Thursday, but largely unrecognised. Borough market Mon-Sat; Westgate Market Mon-Sat (EC Thurs); Piece Hall market Fri and Sat.

Transport: Easily reached via the M62 from Manchester and Leeds. Main line BR station on the Calderdale Line between Manchester and Leeds.

Entertainment: Victoria Theatre, Wards End (01422 351188). Halifax Playhouse, King Cross Street (01422 365998).

Multi-screen Cannon Cinema, Wards End (01422 352000). Square Chapel Arts Centre, Square Road, plus children's theatre season (01422 349422).

IOU Theatre Company — nationally and internationally respected professional touring company, founded on co-operative principles, based at Dean Clough (01422 369217).

Northern Ballet — performances throughout Yorkshire and nationwide (01422 380420).

Sport: North Bridge Leisure Centre (01422 341527). Halifax Swimming Pool, Skircoat Road (01422 366624). Halifax RLFC (rugby league), Thrum Hall (01422 361026).

Halifax Town, league soccer, The Shay (01422 353423). Halifax Golf Club, Ogden (01422 244171).

Orienteering — Two permanent courses, at

Shibden Park and Jerusalem Farm (01422 359454).

Dry ski slope, Halifax Ski Centre, Swalesmoor (01422 340760).

Shows and fairs: Halifax Agricultural Show, Savile Park, second Saturday in August.

Sowerby Bridge rushbearing ceremony. Procession linking local churches, Morris and clog dancing, early September (01422 831896). See also Piece Hall events.

Galleries: Dean Clough Contemporary Art Gallery. Changing exhibitions of work by local and national artists. Open all year, Mon-Sat. Free (01422 357141).

Museums: Eureka! Discovery Road, Halifax. The National Museum for Children, justifiably an award-winner. Spectacular to behold, adventurously designed, extremely well-equipped and enormously popular. The 'museum' is in fact a series of compart-mentalised experiments where children — and adults,

Halifax Parish Church   *V. M. Cockroft-Douglas*

who are allowed in on their own, and obviously love coming to play — can take part, touch, smell, try out and join in. Very noisy, and rather bewildering for small children who don't really get their money's worth.

There are no times when it is not extremely busy, often with school parties, so that access to the equipment is not as easy as it should be. On busy days your visit to the exhibition areas may be restricted to three hours. There are many days when long queues form outside. However it is much cheaper, more educational, better value and unaffected by the weather than any theme park. If the queues look daunting, then try the nearby Industrial Museum instead. Large car park opposite the site, railway station is just next door.

Open daily except Christmas Day. Mon 10-2 (10-5 during school holidays). Wed 10-7. Rest of the week: 10-5. Children (3-12) £3.50. Children under three admitted free. Adults (Over 12) £4.50. Family tickets let in five visitors for £13.50. All visitors are admitted for £1 after 3.30 Tues-Fri during Eureka term time. (01422 330069, or 01422 330012 for details of party bookings.)

Calderdale Industrial Museum, Square Road, adjacent to the Piece Hall. Converted spinning mill, without too much emphasis on 'conversion': this is the reality of working life after the industrial revolution. It smells authentic, the heat can be intense and with only a handful of machines switched on the effect is deafening and frightening.

An excellent educational museum for all ages, but even small children are welcomed, and encouraged to try turning some of the knobs and handles. Highly recommended.

Parking: Use the Sainsbury's car park alongside the Piece Hall, or other town centre car parks. Railway station nearby. Tues-Sat 10-5. Sun 2-5. Closed Mondays except Bank Holidays. Adults £1.50, concessions for children and senior citizens. Under fives get in free (01422 358087).

Piece Hall, Halifax

The Piece Hall. Breathtaking relic of Yorkshire's textile heritage, the Piece Hall is actually a huge square cobbled courtyard surrounded by tiered Italianate colonnaded galleries. The wool merchants of Halifax traded their 'pieces' of cloth here. It was later used as a fruit and vegetable market and then, in the mid-sixties, was spared demolition by one vote on the town council, which had plans for a new car park. Instead the Piece Hall was splendidly restored.

Gallery units now house antique shops, booksellers, candlemakers and purveyors of the tasteful sort of tourist ephemera. To appreciate the architecture it is vital to go on a quiet day — Mondays and Tuesdays, for example. Open markets on Fridays and Saturdays, antiques and flea market on Thursdays, and special markets at Easter and Spring bank holidays. The square is also used for concerts and other events, including the annual Halifax Happening on August Bank holiday Monday.

Use any of the town centre car parks — Sainsbury's is the nearest, but often full. Or come by train.

The building is open all year except Christmas and Boxing Day, 9-6. Opening times of the individual shops vary, but most open 10-5, Tues to Sun. The Piece Hall Art Gallery: Tues-Sun 10-5. The Tourist Information Centre, a couple of cafes and plenty of

Shibden Hall, Halifax   *John Edenbrow*

snack shops are based within the Piece Hall. Free, although there may be a charge for individual festivals and other events (01422 358087).

Bankfield Museum, Boothtown Road. Splendid collection of textiles and costumes, along with displays of local and natural history, set in Akroyd Park. The building also houses the Duke of Wellington's Regimental Museum. Tues-Sat 10-5. Sun 2-5. Closed Mon. Free (01422 354823).

Gardens: Shibden Park and Hall. Early 15th century house, home of a small folklife museum, set in 90 acres of informal parkland with boating lake, cafe, miniature railway, orienteering course. Grounds free, open daily. Hall: March-Nov, MonSat 10-5. Sun 12-5. Feb, Sun only, 2-5. Dec and Jan, closed. Adults £1.50, children and concessions 75p.

Manor Heath demonstration garden. Herb garden, vegetable and fruit gardens, herbaceous border, organic garden, display house. April-Sept, daily 10-4. Oct-March, Sat and Sun 10-4. Free. (01422 365631).

Nearby: Rochdale Canal (see Hebden Bridge).

Smith Art Gallery, Brighouse. Variable opening hours. Free. (01422 719222).

Joseph Dobson's Sweet Factory, Elland. Party visits by prior arrangement to boiled sweet manufacturer (01422 372165).

Tourist Information Centre, Piece Hall (01422 368725).

Holmfirth

Population 23,400. Sturdily attractive mill town, now adopted by the late 20th century art and craft movement, with galleries galore and more than a handful of up-market shops. Ah, but what about the Wrinkled Stocking Tearoom and Sid's Cafe? What on earth do visitors think of Holmfirth if they don't follow television situation comedy? Rare species, evidently, for the town is now almost universally known as the setting for Last of the Summer Wine and the bijou boutiques appear to cohabit comfortably with Nora Batty's house.

The television trippers pour in on Summer Wine coach tours to clog the narrow streets and fill the car parks. Holmfirth is seldom restful, especially in summer, although the steep and narrow ginnels between the weavers' cottages do take pedestrians away from the traffic briefly.

The River Holme, flowing through the town centre, once powered some prosperous mills. It helped destroy some of them too, bursting its banks in three notorious floods now commemorated on plaques and markers around the town.

Shopping: There are still general shops used by locals and visitors alike, in among the galleries (Ashley Jackson paints here), craft shops and second hand bookshops. Also a number of millshops, relics of the textile boom days and now selling good quality clothing at low prices. General market at Crown Bottom, Market Street on Thursdays. Craft market at the same location on Saturdays from Easter to Christmas. Early closing Tuesday, but not all shops.

Transport: Follow the A616 south from Huddersfield. Nearest BR station at Huddersfield. Buses from Huddersfield, Wakefield and Leeds, charter coach tours from just about everywhere in the country.

Shows and fairs: Holmfirth Folk Festival, second week in May, at the Civic Hall and other town centre locations. Details from Tourist Information Centre.

Holmfirth Festival Week, last week in August. Events, games, dances and parades.

Holme Valley Torchlight Procession, late August/early September. Curious evening parade of floats, horses, musicians, from the Old Drill Hall at Thongsbridge to Holmfirth.

Honley Show, early June. Large agricultural and horticultural extravaganza (01484 689306).

Harden Moss sheepdog trials and fell races, late June. Near to Holmfirth on the A635 Greenfield Road is the regular site for this major exhibiting and competitive event (01484 662699/710226).

Holmfirth Art Exhibition, early July (01484 683211).

Galleries: Holmfirth Postcard Museum, Huddersfield Road. Homage to Bamforths, the local firm which pioneered all those saucy seaside postcards. Curiously, they also made some of the very first motion pictures, and you can now see a video presentation of some of their early comedies (1908 to 1914) which used local people as actors. Mon-Sat 10-4, Sun 12-4. £1 adults, 50p children and concessions (01484 682231).

Last of the Summer Wine Exhibition, Huddersfield Road. The inevitable collection of photographs and memorabilia from more than 20 years of the TV series. (You might catch the real thing if filming is taking place — check dates with the Tourist Information Office.) Daily 10-5.30, closed Mondays in winter. Free (01484 681362). Tourist Information Centre, 49-51 Huddersfield Road (10484 687603).

Huddersfield

Population 120,000. Another of West Yorkshire's Victorian textile centres, with some grandiose architecture, and some better forgotten. But where Halifax can be a good place to spend a wet day, Huddersfield in the rain is one of life's forgettable experiences. If you can find your way off the ring road system, the railway station is worth looking at, otherwise you might wish you were back on the ring road.

Shopping: The usual high street chains on a small scale, plus a few slightly more up-market independents. Nicely restored Victorian covered mall, Byram Arcade. Huddersfield has very good markets. The Victorian Brook Street indoor hall hosts a general

Sid's Cafe, Holmfirth

market Mon-Sat. Open market Mon, Thurs and Sat. Bric a brac Tues and Sat (01484 442146). Early closing Weds.

Transport: Just a mile from the M62, and on the main rail link between Liverpool in the west and Hull in the east.

Entertainment: Cannon Cinema, Zetland Street (01484 530874).

Venn Street Arts Centre, repertory theatre and music (01484 430808). Lawrence Batley Theatre and Cellar Theatre, Queen's Square. Recently converted Methodist chapel with ambitious plans and some good local and national drama and dance on offer (01484 430528).

Sport: Huddersfield Town FC league soccer (01484 420335). Huddersfield Rugby League FC (01484 530710). Sports Centre and pool, Old Leeds Road (01484 535231).

Shows and fairs: Huddersfield Contemporary Music Festival, mid-November (01484 425082). Huddersfield Caribbean Carnival, mid-July (01484 539552). Huddersfield Canal Festival, colourful gathering of boats and carnival, early Sept (0161 339 1332).

Galleries: Huddersfield Art Gallery, Princess Alexandra Walk. Large permanent collection representing British art of the last 100 years, including Lowry, Spencer and Hockney. Plus ambitious programme of changing exhibitions by contemporary artists. Mon-Fri 10-5; Sat 10-4. Free. (01484 513808).

Museums: Tolson Memorial Museum, Ravensknowle Park. Victorian mansion in parkland setting (children's play area, crown green bowls, tennis). Displays of textile history, a bit of archaeology, and a good section on transport and travel in the area. There's also a farming exhibition in a restored barn. Mon-Fri 11-5. Sat and Sun 12-5. Free. (01484 530591).

Colne Valley Museum, Golcar. Small but lively and active centre set in restored weavers' cottages, with

Tunnel End, Marsden

working exhibits regularly demonstrated by museum members . You can have a go at spinning, weaving and clog making. Sat, Sun and public holidays, 2-5. Party visits by arrangement. Adults 80p, children and OAPs 40p. (01484 659762).

Nearby: Bagshaw Museum and Butterfly Centre, Wilton Park, Batley. A real gem, one of Yorkshire's great hidden surprises and well worth an hour of any-one's time. It is certainly hidden: first find Batley, and Upper Batley Lane, which runs off the A643, roughly parallel to the A652 Bradford Road. The museum lies at the back of a housing estate, and contains some stunning collections of art from Africa, the Orient, Asia and South America. One gallery sets out to recre-ate the interior of an ancient Egyptian tomb.

The butterfly house is in the museum grounds. Quite small, so wait outside on the lawn until the school parties have done their rounds. Free parking. Mon-Fri 11-5, Sat and Sun 12-5. Free (01924 472514).

Oakwell Hall Country Park, Nutter Lane, Birstall. Well signposted from the A58 Leeds Road, near M62 exit 26. A small and little known late 17th century mansion once owned by a family called Batt and said to be the model for Fieldhead in Charlotte Bronte's 'Shirley'. Well furnished rooms, but don't expect much in the way of period art and craft, and mind the wooden beading across the floor in each doorway.

The vast grounds are used for all sorts of summer events, from horse shows to craft fairs and brass band concerts. The visitor centre and shop staff have details of this really comprehensive programme.

Free parking at two adequate sites, one near the Hall and cafe, the other near to the adventure playground.

Mon-Fri 11-5, Sat and Sun 12-5. Free to the parkland and gardens, £1 to the hall (50p for children, 5-13). Under fives free, but keep them constrained inside the Hall (01924 474 926).

Red House, Oxford Road, Gomersal. After a while you begin to wonder which Yorkshire houses were NOT featured in a Bronte novel. This one is said to be the Briarmains of Charlotte's Shirley, and was actually the home of an early feminist, Mary Taylor. Free parking. Access for disabled visitors to the ground floor of the house only.

March to October, Mon-Fri 10-5, Sat and Sun 12-5. November to February: daily 12-5. Free (01924 872165).

Kirklees Light Railway, Clayton West — narrow (15 in) gauge line built on the route of the old

Oakwell Hall, Birstall

Lancashire and Yorkshire Clayton West branch. Still being developed, but already steam engines link the terminus with the village of Skelmanthorpe. Also model railway — big enough to carry adults — which runs round an ornamental pond, and a model steam traction engine which gives rides in the children's play area. Theme weekends and special events. Daily Easter — end Sept, weekends only otherwise (01484 865727).

Dewsbury Museum of Childhood, Crow Nest Park, Heckmondwike Road, Dewsbury. Small but pleasing displays in an unspectacular stately home. There are the predictable collections of old toys, in glass cases, but also a very good section on 'children at work' in mines, in mills and factories, and on farms. Rather neglected children's play area, with evidence of too many canine visitors and not enough litter bins. Free parking in the grounds. Mon-Fri 11-5, Sat and Sun 12-5. Free (01924 468171).

Tunnel End Canal and Countryside Centre, Marsden. Small museum and interpretation centre set next to Britain's longest and highest canal tunnel. A real treat for the navigation enthusiast. Variable opening times depending on day and season. Free (01484 846062).

Tourist Information Centre, Albion Street, Huddersfield. (01484 687603).

THE GUIDE TEAM

Dalesman's Yorkshire Guide has been produced by a team of researchers, each an expert on their area, to make sure readers get the best possible information on the county.

Terry Fletcher was born in Yorkshire, has spent 25 years recording the life of the county and is Editor of Dalesman, its biggest selling magazine.

John Scott was a journalist in York for almost 40 years and in retirement took an English degree at York University. He has watched and commented on the city's emergence as one of the country's leading tourist centres.

Harry Mead was chief feature writer of the Northern Echo for 24 years and is now a freelance writer. He is the author of Inside the the North York Moors and has contributed to books on Britain's national parks.

Bill Mitchell was Editor of Dalesman for 20 years and was associated with the magazine for almost 40. He has written millions of words about his native county and is the author of more than 100 books.

Eileen Jones is an author and journalist who "adopted" the South Pennines when she settled there in 1980 after working on newspapers and magazines. She is a keen fell runner and unashamed fan of this vibrant area.

Maps by Graeme Park, cover design by David Harkness, layout and production by Paul Jackson